*Dedi

*This book is dea.
Michael and my other two brothers and
two sisters I wanted to let the world
know about the abuse we had to endure,
and how hard we tried to be like other
normal children we had seen around us,
and our struggle for life, we have
survived for.
I would also like to thank Kenneth, my
husband, for his help through the bad
memories of writing this book. My
Daughter Roxanne, and son John just for
being the children that they are, I love
you.*

*For myself, a lot of tears and painful
memories went into this book, being
silent can hurt and leave a lifetime of
emotional scars.*

*Last but not least for my real Father
Henry all of the years that we lost*

together whom I did not get to give or receive hugs from and to tell him that I loved him.

I Love You Daddy!

MY PAST WAS WRITTEN, THE TAKING OF INNOCENCE

A Diary of Child Abuse and Escape

By

Arlene D. Arnold

ISBN: 1-4033-5528-2 (e-book)
ISBN: 1-4033-5529-0 (Paperback)

This book is printed on acid free paper.

1st Books - rev. 08/08/02

Contents

My Name is Arlene

My Past Was Written, The taking of innocence:
This is a true story of Incest, Rape, and Child Abuse

This is a true story about my life as survivor of sexual child abuse, incest and domestic violence.

I wrote this book to let people of incest, child abuse, and domestic violence knowing that you can go on, even though the memories are there, and the healing process can take several years or a lifetime to accomplish the recovery that is necessary for you to go on.

The effects of sexual abuse, such as depression, anger, self-blame may never be recovered, and you may pursue happiness through professional care, such as from a physicians, or crisis counselors, but always remember, you were not responsible for the wrong choices that other people had made for you.

My book is detailed memories of my childhood to adulthood, the age of eighteen, I do remember being three year old so that is where I am starting in with the memories of my life, some of the names were changed for legal purposes.

Some of the details in this book might bother you and for that I am sorry but that was my childhood.

I grew up in a very good neighborhood, and had the potential for many accomplishments in my future, as you will read. Those accomplishments would be just to survive, and as I was trying to survive, dream of a great future, that I would not have, as my future would be written for me. My greatest struggle was to leave the home I was in with some sanity, and my life, because everything else as you will read was pretty much taken from me.

I am a survivor of incest, rape, and child abuse

I am alive, and the scars are there for the rest of my life. I have not gone through any extensive counseling or therapy, for many reasons; Fear of what would happen to my mind, my heart and my body and soul, I want to forget the bad in my past, not my past. It is so much easier to write about what has happen to me than it is to just sit and talk about it. In writing about my past, I would hope that I would let go of the pain that that tortures in my mind with unwanted past memories, which haunt me at the present time.

I am feeling so much stress as my mind starts going back to the past. A strong feeling of hurt as I remember everything clearly and more vivid. I see faces, I hear voices, I hear crying, and I feel pain, my skin crawls every time I hear someone scream in pain.

I am sitting her in my home office staring out at the blue skies; a few rain clouds, bare trees. Trying to stay focused, it is very hard. The month is March, the year 2002. I am living in Klamath Falls, Oregon, where it is still snowing, the tree are bare with little buds on the branches believe it or not, and there is snow on the ground.

It just happens to be the month I was born, March 1st 1961. That year, month or day must have been a curse for me.

Celebrating my birthday has always been a problem for me since I had left home, and the memories, the bad times mostly; I associate my birthday with sadness, the day is very hard to get over until that day has come and gone, then I say to myself I have 364 more days until my birthday comes around again.

A few days before my birthday I get very depressed, nothing makes me happy, it should be a happy occasion; but bad and painful memories are back with a vengeance.

I am married for the third time to a very nice and caring man, his name is Kenneth, but prefers for people to call him Ken except me, that is special, we have been together for about four years.

They have been happy ones except when we speak of family mine in particular.

I have the feeling inside myself that I don't want to be cared for, or I am not worth being cared for, I try my best to push anyone away that cares for me because, I don't want them to hurt nor do I want to inflict pain into their lives, by revealing the pain I had to go through as I was growing up.

Kenneth has been the only person that has taken interest in my childhood, cares about my feelings, and just does not push them aside; we talk about them in the hopes that I will someday let them go, and be happy. Kenneth is very special, and promises that we will always be together no matter how hard things get, he will be there for me, until death us do part.

I try so, so hard to be there for him when he needs me I listen to Kenneth, but sometimes I don't hear him. I find sometimes when he is talking to me about his childhood, which was not great by any means, that I am instantly back in mine, and it is so very hard to come back to reality, sometimes it takes a few days.

I try very hard to focus on other people, people that need my help and then I forget about my life, my pain for a while.

The memories are always on the back burner, I like to say I put them in a filing cabinet in my head somewhere on the bottom shelf behind another cabinet that is hidden.

This book is not focused on color, what race I am, because it can happen in any race, any home rich or poor. That is what I want you the reader to see and focusing on.

The Last Letter

May is the person that had gave birth to me. In the book I will call her May her first name, I do not nor will I recognize her as a mother or my mother. I have not really been in touch with May for almost 20 years.

I believe that May gave up the right to be called mom or mother after years of abuse and allowed abuse.

This is my thoughts on what a mother is; A mother gives of her heart, filled with joy, protects her children from all evil to the best of her abilities, encourages the child to go on when the child feels down. A mother fixes your bumps and bruises with tender loving care, educates you on a positive future.

A mother tells you that you are loved, and always reminds you so you have no doubts, and shows it, last but not least respects you for who you are and who you will become, as I have seen these affections given by parents over the years, most being very caring, as I watched and listened, and even witnessed their love.

May has never shown the ability to have any of these characteristics as a mother; she had never shown that she had even wanted children. Children are and should be a privilege to have; there are so many unlucky people unable to have children in this world.

Yet, some people that have children and mistreat them did not deserve them at all, and should have just put them up for adoption to a caring loving family. Give the children a chance at life.

Well, I wrote to May earlier this year to ask for my photo albums, pictures of me, my images, pictures of myself that were taken while I was in school and growing up through the years. I would like to show them to my husband, as he has been the only one curious of what I looked like when I was a little girl, all of the pictures, pictures of the face of that little girl that had to go through so much pain.

I have just received a letter from May. She had replied with riddles, no answers to any of the questions that I have asked, about my photo albums, only that they had been placed in storage and she did not know when she would be able to give them to me, if ever.

A trigger of bad memories, flashes of meanness and cruelty, chills all over my body. I just started to write, write everything I can remember about my childhood, I thought this might help me and others like myself, show that conquering the haunting demons of your past can be hard, but with determination it can be done.

Domestic Violence

<u>Domestic violence</u> happens when one or several members of a household harms another member or members of the household. It is usually a control issue, and it can be emotional or physical in nature. Domestic violence includes: punching, slapping, pushing, choking, and beatings with whatever device that is handy for them to use at that given time, also can include name-calling, threats, put-downs, and deprivation.

The victim can be a child or children, a parent, or an elder person living in the home, domestic violence knows no limits. Adults who are violent may hurt their children without meaning to, not knowing their own strength. They may also do it to satisfy them selves because of something that had occurred during the day or evening, triggering a violent emotion, leading to a violent act.

Many children growing up in violent or sexual abuse homes may have some of these disorders, as I did, disorders that can be treated medically;

1. High levels of stress, rashes, stomachaches, headaches, ulcers,

diarrhea, or bed-wetting are just some disorders.

2. Unable to have the ability to feel badly for other people, unable to show emotions.
3. Slow development, mentally and physically.
4. Disorders in speech.
5. Lacking trust, toward their parents, in all adults, friends, and even strangers.
6. Withdrawing into any activity to distance them selves from the outside world.
7. Feelings of guilt and very low self-esteem.
8. A feeling that the child has no safe place to go.
9. Unable to concentrate, which can lead to failure school, or any activity the child is attempting.

About Incest

Incest is

Incest is; intercourse between people who are too closely related. It also includes other sexual acts such as fondling, molestation, and exhibitionism, Sexual abuse, incest includes, showing a child pornographic materials, placing the child's hand on another person's genitals, touching a child's genitals, and/or penetration of any orifice of a child's body (mouth, vagina, anus) with a penis, finger, or an object of any sort. Penetration does not have to occur for it to be sexual abuse.

Incest is not; Normal physical affection between parents and children, like holding hands, hugs; kisses and horse play. Without healthy affection, parents and children alike will miss much of the warmth and security that is intended for family members to have with each other.

In my case my step-dad was the offender, but can often be another family members, such as close family friend, uncles, aunts and so on can also falls into this category because of the child's trusting relationship with them, a lot of the time it will be the stepfather.

Sexual abuse happens in families of every economic and ethnic background, not just among the poor, but rich alike. Many molesters appear to be upstanding members of their community like May pretended to be. Sadly, most cases go unreported, so the full extent of this problem remains hidden.

Of the known sexual abuse seventy five percent is committed by the children's own parents or someone well trusted close to the family. The victims are young boys and girls between the ages of eight and twelve, and the other twenty five percent under the age of seven.

In my case I believe that both parents knew incest was going on in the home and one over looked the others abuse hidden only from outsiders. We were abused, and programmed into what was right for their needs. When the abuse was over by both parents, it left lifetime scares, the one parent that still tries to contact me says she did nothing wrong, and has the nerve to ask the question, what did I do?

About Rape, Sexual Assault

Rape is a Sexual Assault, forcible sodomy (oral copulation with a member of the opposite or same sex), and forcible sexual penetration (to enter by forcible overcoming resistance), of another person's oral, anal or genital opening with any object, and these acts are committed without consent. Touching an unwilling person's intimate parts (defined as genitalia, groin, breast, or buttocks, or the clothing covering them) or forcing an unwilling person to touch another's intimate parts for the purpose of gratifying the sexual desire of either party These acts are committed without consent and by force, threats, and intimidation, or victim's mental or physical helplessness. This would include the inability to consent due to excessive alcohol, drug use or mental illness or being totally incapacitated.

Rape is:

1. *Force of any sexual act with an unwilling participant.*
2. *Forcible sexual penetration.*
3. *Sex without consent.*

4. *Sex while the partner is incapacitated, sleeping or otherwise.*

5. *Inability to consent to sex due to excessive alcohol*

6. *Mentally ill, (don't have the all of their faculties) and have the Inability to Consent.*

7. *Threats of violence if you do not comply with the act of rape.*

8. *There are many more situation, I have only list a few common scenarios*

9. *(For more info on all four subjects, Domestic Violence, Incest, Rape, Sexual Assault, Please contact your local hospital, local police department, or a rape counselor hotline.)*

Pittsburg, CA. 1961

A little history of the area

Located at the point where the Sacramento and San Joaquin rivers meet. The earliest recorded history of the town starts in the year 1839 when the Mexican government granted almost 10,000 acres to Jose Antone Mesa and Miguel Jose Garcia. Pittsburg was part of a big land purchase in 1849 and first known as New York Landing. Lieutenant William Tecumseh Sherman as New York Of The Pacific surveyed the town. Following the survey discovery of coal in the hills three miles south of town, the town was renamed Black Diamond in 1903, Thriving in coal mining, fishing and the canning industries. Finally, the name changed to Pittsburg, after the famous steel mill in the Pennsylvania.

(For more info on Pittsburg, Ca, please go to you local library.)

My birth certificate

I wish I could really remember what happen the day I was born but I can't, I have a record of birth to prove that I am here and that I was born but I am constantly asking myself what was I put on this earth for? Pittsburgh, Calif. 1961. A time you never asked question you did what you were told or you were punished, beat whipped, however you would like to call it, it was abuse as it was in my family. A time of fear if you spoke anything negative to anyone outside your family. I feared for my life. Who would believe you if your parents pretended to be someone they were not.

My birth father Alex, whom I love and respect with all my heart, named me Arlene;

the source of the name is an Irish Gaelic expression meaning "Pledge or promise." I was born on Wednesday, March 01, 1961 at 3:21 am.

As of Thursday, April 25, 2002 I am 41 years old and have lived 15030 days, surprisingly.

In 1961 John F. Kennedy is inaugurated President of the United States. An estimated 1,200 anti-Castro exiles aided by U.S. make a failed invasion of Cuba's Bay of Pigs. Navy Cmdr.

Alan B. Shepard Jr. becomes the first U.S. spaceman after rocketing 118 miles above the earth.

Hurricane "Carla" wipes out Texas gulf cities claiming 46 lives. Russian Cosmonaut Yuri Gagarin makes the first manned space flight.

I am Pisces, and Pisces are sensitive to psychological issues and whatever is beneath the surface. This comes from their emotional and yet understanding, yet imaginative nature. Their inner goals are very important which makes them forgiving of any negative environment. Pisces are giving of themselves for the sake of more important issues.

Arlene D. Arnold

Sacramento, Ca

Sacramento Info.

Sacramento is the capitol of California, and is the largest city in the valley.

The valley bears the Spanish name for the "Holy Sacrament," a name first applied to the Feather River by Gabriel Moraga in 1808.

Wheat farming dominated the valleys economy in the 1860s and 1880s. Improvements in Wheat farming, such as irrigation and transportation led to an abundance of various crops, including the raising of apricots, apples, apricots, pears, barley, alfalfa, and safflower.

The official California State Flower is the Golden Poppy, which in 1913 the legislature adopted the Golden Poppy as the California State Flower, brilliant orange petals blooming from March through May on hill and valleys across California.

California State Tree is the Sequoia sempervirens, which in 1953 became the official California State Tree. Redwoods are the world's tallest trees, some having reached a height of more than 360 feet or more.

My Past Was Written, The Taking of Innocence
(For more info on Sacramento, please visit your local library.)

Arlene D. Arnold

I can remember being three years old living in Sacramento, Ca

I was born in a small town of Pittsburg, CA. but my home would be in Sacramento, Ca. until I was four years of age.

I am ***three years old*** everything seems to be so huge to me as I am about two and a half feet tall. This is me, an image of what I looked like I have long light brown wavy hair; very light skin tone I am very energetic and very curious as a child my age usually is.

I am walking barefoot on a polished hardwood floor through out the house, the walls are lime green in the living room and they are newly painted I can still smell the paint as if it was still wet.

The curtains in the large living room were white with fringe around them that covers the entire window.

I hear a washer humming and the water swishing back and forth, it looks like a very old washer with a wringer device above it that I like to play with. I can climb up the step stool and look in the washer there is no lid I just like standing there watching the clothes go back and forth. I get down off the step stool, walk to the kitchen.

I smell bacon cooking, I walk into the kitchen and in the center of the kitchen is a metal-framed kitchen table and chairs. I climb up on a chair to see the stovetop; the stove is white old fashion looking with a grill in the middle where the bacon is frying, I really wanted a piece of bacon but the stove was just too hot.

The kitchen is yellow with only one window, which is covered with yellow floral curtains above an old porcelain sink. There are many cabinets around the sink and way above the sink, all yellow. I get down from the chair and go to my bedroom.

No, it's not lime green it's light blue there are two twin beds and a dresser in the middle.

Well, anyway I came in here to find my brother Brad whom is two years older than I am and almost a head taller than me. His skin tone is dark; he has short black frizzy hair just like my May.

Brad is getting ready for school. I want to go with him so badly; I don't want to stay at home. I hear May's voice from the living room, it time for school you don't want to be late Brad.

I get to give Brad a big hug before he goes, I have to stay in the house, watch him from the inside of the screen door, crying. Brad walks across the street, through a gate; he is there, in the Kindergarten playground.

May is the person that gave birth to me my biological mother. She stands about five feet three inches her hair is black, which she wares up most of the time. Her skin is dark, I compare it to mine, kind of like dark brown sugar and light brown sugar, or black coffee with a little cream, and me coffee with lots of cream.

Well any way, that's what the woman that has given birth to me looks like. She wears dresses all of the time no pants, I never seen her in pants until I was older. I look at her now, and then, she had many dresses like Lucy, a comedian from the fifties era.

The Bathroom is mildew smelling as I watch the bathtub fill with water and bubbles. The bathtub is white, has feet very old fashion; the sink is white porcelain just like the bathtub. The sink has metal poles holding it up in front. The floor has black and white linoleum; there is a tiny window over the bathtub, and a small mirror over the sink.

May walks into the bathroom starts yelling it's bath time it's time for our bath Michael and me whom is my younger brother by one year. He has long straight black hair, same skin tone as me.

Michael does not say much just a few words like mama, dada, food, and candy, drink that's about it. We get to do everything together, even bathe, that meant lots of bubbles I loved bubble baths.

We both have so much fun with the bubbles throwing them up in the air, blowing them, making beards and mustaches, and hiding our bath toys under the bubbles.

I can remember many times my stomach was hurting and before I could get into the bath and play in the bubbles with Michael, I had to have an enema. I never understood why this was happening to me, at that age I did not understand too much.

May was sitting on the toilet seat; I was laying across her lap my stomach touching her knees.

A bulb syringe in a sink full of water and bubbles was filled and on the tip of the bulb syringe Lubricant was place on the tip and slowly it was place inside me, not once, but it felt like my stomach was going to pop, she would say over and over hold it, hold it. I was sat on the toilet and allowed to go to the bathroom my stomach hurt more and then less and less.

I could now take a bath, that is all I wanted to do, at that age I was not too bothered by what May was doing to me, all I knew is when it was done I was in pain for a while, then the pain would be gone.

I do remember seeing her give my other brothers and sister enemas from time to time, but not as frequently as me.

My sister Brenda is a year old, I don't see her much, she sleeps a lot still and sometime she is in her playpen.

She is also very light skinned, with short brown frizzy hair cries a lot, noisy, smile.

We don't do much but play with our toys take naps, eat and then it is bedtime. Everyday is pretty much the same; the best part of the day was when Daddy walks in the door about 6:30 at night, almost bedtime.

My father's name is Alex he's a very busy working in concrete construction. Dad is pretty much never home to me because we go to bed before he arrives a lot of the time.

Well, now it is bedtime six-thirty in the evening Dad just walked in and there is chaos, joyful hellos, happy hugging as we tell daddy how much he was missed all day.

Dad stands about six feet tall, black straight hairs, thin build, blue eyes, and very light skinned compared to May.

All of the children are jumping on dad giving kisses and hugs before bedtime, May saying "bedtime, bedtime" the whole time we are with Dad, almost like she was jealous of the time we were taking away from the both of them, we would finally then go to bed.

I can remember waking up many times in the middle of the night my leg in agonizing pain from my hip to my ankle.

May would bring in a thermometer with Lubricant on it I was to lay on my stomach and the thermometer was placed in my bottom and then taken out, I had no fever, but if I did I would have had a fever, aspirin would be place inside my bottom.

My leg would be wrapped with an ace bandage from the top of my thigh down to my ankle and then I went to sleep, feeling the throbbing pain off and on all night. This would happen many, many times as I was growing up I never thought too much of it.

After we had gone to bed May and Dad would sit down and have diner, May never sat and ate dinner with us until we were older, nine is the age I recall May sitting down and eating with us as a family.

May was now getting heavier, her stomach was getting much bigger and dad would say to me May is going to have a baby it is going to be a little boy how did he know?

A few months had gone by and May came home from the hospital with a little baby brother, I was happy I have another little baby brother David. David looks a lot like my older brother Brad, his hair black and frizzy, and his skin tone dark just like May's.

To keep from waking up my little brother and sister we played outside most of the morning on a clear day and when it rained we played in the living room quietly.

Brad likes to stay in and watch TV when he comes home from school everyone else is taking naps. My new little brother is very quiet, he never cries.

I was playing outside with Michael we were out in the backyard there was big slab cement standing freely. We were told not to get upon the cement it just looked like it would be fun to climb on, Michael climbed up on the three foot, four inch wide slab it was starting to rock and fell over.

Michael was now half way under the slab, screaming, and crying I ran in the to house yelling Michael is hurt.

May had ran outside and then back inside to call for help the Fire Department whom was now here, pulling the cement off of Michael,

He was very hurt badly I was crying and scared Michael was not crying anymore. The ambulance took him to the hospital. I did not get to see Michael for two weeks while he was in the hospital. He had two broken legs and pelvic bone. He was in a body cast when he came home.

I would sit in the bedroom with Michael all of the time, or where ever he was moved in the house I would ask him does it hurt, he would say no, he could not move around at all. I could not wait until he was up and out of the cast. We would watch TV together play games, such as talking games little kids would play, such as what color I had wrote on a piece of paper, how many fingers do I have and so on. Michael was almost three years old now, very talkative more that he was at the beginning of his second birthday.

My **fourth birthday** was celebrated in the bedroom with Michael, while he lay in bed with his body cast on. May had baked a white cake with blue frosting. Arlene, my name, on the top of the birthday cake, and Michael's name at the bottom, and seven candles in the middle, me blowing out the candles for the both of us.

It seemed like months be before Michael and I were able to go out and play. A whole year has gone by, I am four years old.

Still not old enough to for school. I can honestly say at the age of three I was somewhat happy. If that is what happiness was. No spankings, not yelled at, just to play eat and take naps.

May was pregnant, again

I started seeing people I have never seen before coming in and out of the house I was told by May, this is your Dads brother and some other people that I can't remember, I was confused, why are these men here and dad has to work or just not be home with us?

One morning I remember waking up and going to May's bedroom. My little sister Brenda and David were in there laying in bed with May whom was naked and a guy that looked somewhat similar to my father, but it was not my Dad. He was naked no blankets or sheets on him or on May, they both never told us to leave the room, the both of them seemed rather happy to see us in the room with the both of them. May's stomach was very big she was telling me this is where the baby is, and showing us where the baby would be coming from.

The guy that looked like dad was just lying there was rubbing himself his hands on his penis, I looked and pointed as May watched the man say to me, touch this meaning his penis I did it was hard with a soft skin over it.

29

He said this is what makes babies he then said lick it I licked it once and it tasted very nasty then I watched him as he kept rubbing himself, white cream came out of the tip of his penis and went all over he then

Left the bed and went into the bathroom May would say for us to go watch TV until she could get up and make breakfast.

Later the same evening, I can't remember if any of us children said something to Dad when he came home from work but there was yelling by both May and my daddy after we had gone to bed and the next day daddy didn't come home from work May then would say to us your dad is no longer going to be coming home at night anymore. What happened and why is he not coming home? Daddy I miss you.

Dad would now come over on the weekends to pick up Brad, my older brother Michael my younger brother and me and we would go fishing that was so much fun. Just spending time with my daddy was all that I really wanted I sure did miss him a lot at home. I now was able to see so much more of my Dad he never had taken us out before he was always working. I remember going to breakfast with Dad and my older brother Brad and Michael on the mornings Dad would pick us up.

This was a really nice we would drive to a home walk upstairs and be greeted by a very nice lady whom would always ask how we were, take our jackets and hang them up. We would then sit at the table in the kitchen and talk to this nice lady for while she would make breakfast for all of us we would eat then go fishing with dad, the lady never went with us, it would have been nice if she did, I liked her. This lasted for about four months.

May would ask about this woman when we returned home an all I could say is that she was nice and she cooks breakfast like you May and then we go fishing with dad. May seemed to be upset after she would ask us all of these questions she would go to the living room and sit on the couch and cry.

There was nothing I could do I didn't know what or why these things were happening I had asked time and time again after each visit with daddy. Is daddy coming home I would ask May I was told to go away and play with my brothers and sister my first feelings of rejections.

I did notice that May was pregnant as her stomach was growing more and more and daddy was not there to see this like he was with my baby brother, I wondered if I was going to have a little sister or another little brother.

A month later I would meet my grandfather Henry on my dad side of the family for the first time he looked very much like my father, but just a little older he was very light skinned with short black straight hair, blue eyes with a foreign French accent. Grandpa was born and raised in France until he was a teenager about fourteen years old desperately wanting to leave France and come to the United States stowed away on a ship to America.

Grandpa grew up here in the states and made it into the history books as one of the builders of the Panama Canal after that he would settle down and raise a family, at the time I meet him he would be in his sixties.

Grandfather stood about five foot eight, he had a bad limp from an accident he had earlier in his life with a forklift on the docks of San Francisco.

This was not a happy time May was crying to Grandpa she had said that she wanted to leave our home in Pittsburg, CA. she told my grandfather about the other woman that my dad would take us to see.

That was a day I remember for the rest of my life so vividly like it was yesterday daddy was standing there, in front of our home as we were being shoved in Grandpa's car a black and white Cadillac screaming and crying. Grandpa was telling Dad to stay away from his children and May. Brad put up a fight franticly he holding on to my daddy's legs and my grandfather grabbing Brad and putting him in the car as we were told to stay inside.

We were packed into in the back seat packed like sardines the smaller kids on the laps of the bigger kids, as the older kids were crying May sitting in the front seat and my grandfather was in the driver seat.

The car would start moving Dad had tears in his eyes he started crying out loudly please don't do this please I love my children, I want to stay with daddy I had said over and over again as did Michael and Brad whimpering and crying.

With no sympathy at all by May or our grandfather the car would be moving faster, daddy was getting smaller, further and further away and I watched him drop to his knees, then I could no longer see him any more. I cried so much I was tired, my head hurt and then I fell asleep. Menlo park, CA. is the location we would be moving to.

Arlene D. Arnold

A Little History of Menlo Park, and Atherton California

Menlo Park & Atherton CA.

Menlo Park

In 1854 Menlo Park received its official name when two Irishmen, D. C. McLean and Dennis J. Oliver, whose wives were sisters, purchased 1,700 acres bordering County Road, now known as the El Camino Real.

Two houses were built with one entrance leading into the property. When entering the property you would see the name *Menlo Park* with the date of, August 1854, below the bold letter their name.

The railroad came through in 1863, the station just did not have a name, and it was just the end of the line.

There would be a discussion of the name, one of the officials had glanced over the gate nearest the railroad, and had seen the sign *Menlo Park* that is what the official name would become This station is now California State Landmark No. 955, the oldest California station in continuous operation today.

The population of Menlo Park is 32,000 currently, and it is approximately thirty miles south of San Francisco. Some places in Menlo Park are; St. Michael's Seminary, Corpus Christi Monastery, Menlo College, Sacred Heart, and more. Nearing cities, within a half to three miles are Atherton, Palo Alto, Woodside, to name a few, and approximately two miles to Stanford University.

(For more information, please go to the Menlo Park library or contact The Menlo Park Historical Association)

Atherton

The San Francisco, San Jose Railroad In 1866 had a flag stop for the affluent owners, Fair Oaks- Atherton whom owned the large estates who lived just north of Menlo Park. It was decided to honor Faxton Dean Atherton who had been one of the first property owners in the south peninsula and name the Town for him. Atherton was incorporated on September 12, 1923.

Atherton purchased 640 acres for ten dollars an acre in 1860. Atherton built his home years later, large enough for his growing family, of which he had seven children altogether.

Faxton Dean Atherton a native of Massachusetts, Atherton first came to the Pacific coast in 1834 for the purpose of trading. In 1840

He settled in Valparaiso and became a successful merchant, becoming one of the wealthiest men on the Pacific coast. In 1860 Atherton moved to California, he sold his assets from his prior estate and reinvested his money in California. The land that was purchased is now known as Atherton.

(For more information, please go to the Atherton library, or contact the San Mateo County Historical Association)

Strange Place

The town is Menlo Park, California where I would call home now on and off for the next seventeen years. There were redwood, and oak trees everywhere. A large white Victorian style two story home built in 1910. Six foot Green hedges that surround the front of the house, many flowers and roses with a giant redwood tree, one of the tallest in the area.

As we pulled into the driveway, there were green beans growing on a vine right next to the house.

A little further down the driveway there were blackberry bushes to your right a garage straight ahead and to your left apple, apricot, plum, and Chinese plum trees, near the patio was many varieties of roses.

We had finally come to a stop grandpa saying for us to get out of the car. We had just woke up after such a long drive and already bad memories of leaving my father behind I was use to being at home running around and playing not cramped sitting in the car.

Grandpa told us not to touch anything he was not use to having kids around his home he was telling May that we made him very nervous. He told us to go to the patio and sit down while he and May went into the house, my brothers and sisters and me just looked at each other and said nothing and a few minutes' later May and grandpa came out with a pitcher of juice and glasses.

On our street there were five homes all of them looking the same, grandpa's would be the only two story home and right down the street was a lumberyard and about a half a block further was a liquor store.

Directly across the El Camino Real was a co-ed college behind the college was a boys school which was a high school nine though twelve were the grades the school started and ended at, directly behind the boy's high school was Sacred Heart School for girls.

About three miles from our home was Stanford University hospital and college near there was Stanford shopping center. Coming back to our area, depending on which direction you took, was Atherton, a very rich community. Beautiful mansions, which were very large and very well, kept, most of the mansions behind Flood Gates Estate.

It was a very warm day outside about one in the afternoon the month was June the roses and flowers smelled like perfume, we must have sat outside for about three hours, just us children.

May had walked outside the back door and stood on the porch steps and she would say, it is time to come in, don't touch anything. I had thought in my mind of four years old, what would happen if we did?

Would we melt, or maybe disappear, I never found out I never touched a thing inside the home. One at a time we walked into the house, as I walked in I smelled strange odor I can't really place the smell.

I walked from the porch to the kitchen, everything clean and shinny, the kitchen was big and well taken care of, bigger then what I was accustom. As I looked around I saw a wooden kitchen table for two with wooden chairs, upper and lower wooden stained cabinets, a porcelain sink and a stainless steel stove top, and a stainless steel double door oven as you turned around.

This was a much nicer kitchen than we had at home, from there we walked through the kitchen doorway and there was the dining room, beautiful with many antique furnishings.

When you entered the room there would be two glass china cabinets, one cabinet filled with china, plates, cups with gold trim, and the other with crystal glassware. The wood on the cabinets was dark; it matched the dining table, which was about eight feet long with high back fancy chairs and a chandelier above the table. The floor had a dark Asian style carpet that fit the whole room. There was only one large window in the room with lace white curtains.

We were asked by May to sit at the table because your Grandpa was making something to eat and she was going to get the bedrooms ready for us we had stew, bread and butter and juice, watching I did not see where Grandpa had gone he did not eat with us and neither did May.

It was now time to get ready for bed we bathed and were now ready for bed. The bathroom was old fashion looking compared to the modern home we were living in previously. A cast iron porcelain covered tub with feet, old porcelain sink, the toilet looked new, the floor had wood with a white fluffy rug, a linen closet and a small window that let the smell of the flowers outside come in.

We now were ready to see were we are going to sleeping, from the bathroom we walk a short distance into a hallway that had crushed velvet red and burgundy wallpaper with an old design, we started walking up stairs you could hear the boards squeak under our feet as we slowly ascended up the stairs the carpet on the stairs a deep dark red color matching the wallpaper.

We were half way up and made a sharp turn to go up the next flight of stairs, we all held on to the wooden banister to go the rest of the way upstairs.

May said we're here, as we walked into a room there was three twin beds where Brad would sleep in one, I shared mine with Brenda, Michael and David shared the other one. May would be in the bedroom next to ours. We had a very big day and we all quickly fell asleep quickly.

Here is a floor plan of the house.

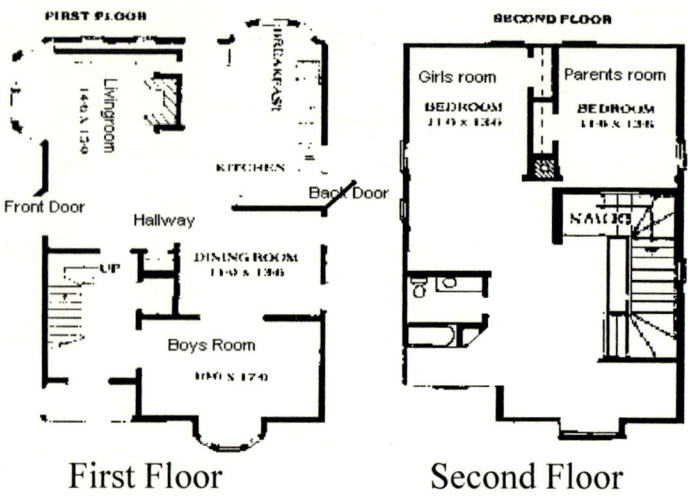

First Floor   Second Floor

It is now morning and we are up putting on our clothes, running down stairs to wash up and eat breakfast. I could hear my Grandpa saying in a rather loud tone of voice that he does not want young kids running around the house, tearing up house that took him a lifetime to build for him and his wife, right then and there I just knew that he did not like us and did not want us around.

I was really quiet after hearing that I wondered what was going to happen to myself and my brothers and sister. We were made to go outside and play for most of the day, eat lunch out on the patio, which was peanut butter and apple butter jam sandwiches; dinner was in the house at six thirty every day, which would last for two weeks, then the fun was over, never to have fun again.

The next day for breakfast was oatmeal, no sugar, or cream as what grandpa was accustom, didn't believe in sugar or cream in cereal. It tasted awful, not what we were use to. Even though, we did eat the cereal because we were hungry, then was able to get up and go outside to help pull weeds, we were given sections to pull, and there was no talking allowed.

For diner one night I could remember having spaghetti for dinner one night, it was very spicy and somewhat hot as my grandpa liked spicy foods, it just did not agree with my stomach, I was sick, the food came back up and on to my plate it went. Well, as disgusting as in now looked and smelled I was not allowed to get up from the table until I ate every bit of the food on my plate. In my mind, I was just begging and pleading with God for his help, no help came for me.

May, said nothing in my defense to help me, as a mother should have, she as well as my grandfather just watched as this must have amused them maybe, or this was part of the lesions, teaching I would have to endure. I ate the last bite of spaghetti on my plate; I was chocking and gagging on every mouthful, until the plate was empty. Let me say, to this day I hate spaghetti; I can't even look at it with out feeling ill.

After finishing thc food I was allowed to get up and go to the bathroom, where they had both stated, this is where you get sick, not at the table.

I sat in front of the toilet leaning over the bowl throwing up, my throat was burning and the smell was making me more ill as if I would never finish and be able to get up. This must of lasted about twenty minutes or more I washed out my mouth over and over again to get rid of the taste it just would not go away.

The abuse of not being able to eat the foods that my grandfather was accustomed to would go on for many months to come I was sick a lot; I really started to know the toilet bowl like a close friend.

A few days would pass and during that time May had another baby a little girl name Annie a baby sister, she looks so much like a doll her skin tone like mine, brown curly hair, and wide eyes, dressed in pink. Now that makes six children all together.

May is asking Grandpa what is she going to do with six kids and no father to raise them I would then say out loud I have a dad that was the first time I remember getting yelled at, I was made to sit on the floor in a corner.

I sat for a long time I started to fall asleep and again my Grandpa yelled me saying that he would go out and get a switch off the tree and use it on my bottom, I looked at him and started to cry. He then started yelling at May, do something with your kids or you will have to find somewhere else to live.

May started to yelling more she even started to swat us with her hands, there was no talking allowed in the house since Grandpa was use to the house being quiet.

An older woman walked into the room from Grandpa's bedroom, I had never seen her before. May introduced us to her saying this is you Grandmother she worked very early in the morning, and came home after we had gone to bed this was her day off Grandmother did not say much at all. She was dark skinned like May, with white long hair down to her waist, very thin, maybe a hundred pounds.

I remember my grandmother to be a very nice lady she had made me dry my tears one day when I was sitting on the back steps crying and said there is nothing that bad to make such a pretty little girl cry. I liked her very much grandpa was not so mean and grumpy when Grandmother was around.

Five years old

I was now *five years old*, I don't even remember having a birthday party, I think it just came and went, overlooked the same as my other brothers and sisters no party or celebrating of being a year older. All I knew was that I am old enough to go to school with my older brother Brad.

We were now shopping at big named stores for school clothes trying on many clothes, I remember bring home many shopping bags of clothes home.

It is now September I remember getting ready for school with Brad, I was very excited to be going to school, I wanted to know the fun that Brad was having when he was away from about seven hours a day.

Michael was crying just like I use to when I saw Brad go off to school, now I did not want to go, I wanted to stay home with Michael so he did not feel so bad. I was taken to school any way my new school was the school I attended was Encinal School-195 Encinal Ave Atherton, CA 94027. Brad was first to class as May walked us through the school.

He was not scared at all I did not see him for the rest of the day until he came home on the school bus, now it was my turn.

I first saw the playground and I was so excited to go play, and then I saw about thirty other kids standing around with their parents, a lot of them were crying and that's when I started to get scared. I wanted to hold May's hand and never let it go. I was introduced to the kindergarten teacher Mrs. Moingham, and then May said I have to go now and I started to cry and hold on to May's hand tighter.

The teacher grabbed my other hand and said lets go meet some of the other children, as May pulled her had away, right at that moment I did not feel her love, nor did I feel the May would protect me from evil or anything else that would happen in my life.

It seemed to get easier to go to school on a daily basis, I started to make friends, Sheila, Lisa, Cheryl, Scott, friends that I wanted to see every day and play with, the playing was almost forbidden now at home. Don't touch this or that, don't go in here or there, don't talk was now the language at home. School was now freedom to be myself until I went home. I did feel sorry for my brother and sisters that had to stay at home, because I did not have to hear nothing negative for at least four hours a day while being at school.

I would come home from school just to be yelled at by May's and her father, they would say put on your work clothes, there is no time for play here. When you walk into this house it is time to clean, so that is what we did every day.

I was instructed to get on my hands and knees with a bucket, starting from the top of the stairs, washing the red carpet and wiping it dry, each and every stair until I reached the bottom. I would have chores like that every day. I was on my knees cleaning inside or out pulling weeds or cleaning the floor the problems seemed to be worsening here at home. I heard my Grandpa yelling at us all of the time now, he was just not happy, nor was I or my brothers and sisters.

I was scared to be living here in this home children are suppose to fell security, and be in a loving atmosphere, have some sort of joy, or so I thought.

I thought of my dad a lot missing him just wishing I would be able to see him that maybe he would come and pick us up and take us home with him. I could remember my father's face somewhat and a kind generous smile he would never be cruel or mean, never.

The year was now at end and school was out for the summer. On the last day of school I remember telling the friends that I had made in school, I would see them when school started again, that would not be true.

I had come home from the last day of school; I entered the house to find that my baby sister and youngest brother were not there.

I asked May where Annie and David were, May replied I sent them to a foster home, I am unable to take care of all of you right now. Brad and Michael are leaving tomorrow and the following day you and Brenda will be going.

I asked if that was because Grandpa did not like us, May replied, I need time to straighten out my life, this is his house and he does not like the change of having children around, which is why you are leaving.

I asked what about dad? Can I go and stay with him May replied you are never to mention your father ever again, he is a terrible man and he does not love you, his name is not allowed in this house period. She would go on to say, he never wanted you or you're other brothers and sisters. He is a liar a cheat and a thief, and then she would often finish her sentences with a question, do you want to be around someone like that?

What an obscene statement May had just made to me I have no answer to the twisted question I was asked. Being all of five years old what was I to know about what May was talking about. My father as I knew him was a good man not a thief what was a thief anyway?

A liar? I knew what the word lying meant as explained to me by my father but never did I see my father as a liar in my eyes.

A cheat what was that? Why would May go on and say so many horrible and disrespectful things about my father and what did she know if anything differently? I could remember when May and my father would sit and hold hands, and my dad would always give her hugs and kisses.

What happened and why was May such a mean spirited speaker when it came to my father? May would often use the word hate whenever she spoke of my father or used his name, was May rejected or did she reject my father.

The real question was what did she do to make him stop loving her, and for May to start rejecting her children? We would never hear the correct reason from May she was never at fault for anything she did or said.

I still loved my father no matter what was said, he never caused me any pain, he had always shown me love as he did for my other brothers and sisters. I was also told there was a court order for my father never to come and see us, I did not understand that either. She was punishing him as well as us children; we needed our father in our lives I will see my dad again one day in the future, one day.

I am now **six years old**, and still no birthday party to celebrate getting older nor for the rest of my brothers and sisters either. What happened? Why did everything change? What happiness there was in our little lives has changed. Our family was not a family any more, it was being torn apart.

My clothes are packed and ready to go along with my younger sister Brenda's. I notice a car pulling into the driveway as I am looking out of the front window a woman gets out of the car walks to the front door and May answers it. The woman had asked for us by name May had come inside grabbed our suitcases and walked us to the door, no hug or kisses on the cheek not even a good-bye. We walk down the stairs down the walkway to the driveway and we were asked to get into the car.

Twenty minutes of driving and we pull into a driveway of a one level home. In front of the house stood a couple in their early fifties, they are both light skinned people, the older man had a pot belly and white hair, as a matter of fact so did the older lady. They both seem very happy to see my sister and me.

We came in and were shown our room unpacked and went out to play, wow I thought, there is toys to play with and nobody is yelling at us for talking. I missed my brothers and sisters, I wondered if I would see them again.

The Foster Home

Foster homes and foster parents are ordinary people, heroes to a lot of children, which come from abusive homes. People who open their hearts and homes to children whose families are in crisis, as mine was. Foster parents provide, temporary care and safety for the children until a family can be successfully reunited.

Before being placed in a foster home I always though that this was a place you would go if you were unwanted or your parents had died, something like that. Kind of like orphanage living I guess. Why are parents so quick just to throw a child away when things are not going well for them? The child did not ask to come into this world, not to be uncared for, not to be loved, not to be treated like an animal, or even sometime worse.

The family that was to take care of us was very nice I did not have to worry about hearing May and my grandfather argued. A few days of being at this new home I did not feel nervous, and my stomach stopped hurting me.

I liked both foster parents a lot; they had been married for a long time and they cared about one another I could see that with my own eyes a kiss here a peck there and holding hands. My foster mother had said she would talked to me like I was one of her own daughters I felt so comfortable with her.

I remember my foster mother combing my hair telling me one day I would grow up to be such a beautiful and a wonderful mother and a great wife for some special man, she said that with her heart.

After a few days had past my foster mother asked me if I missed being at home, I told her that I missed my brothers and sisters I did not miss the arguing yelling and screaming, which really scared me.

While sill on the same subject I also told her some of the things that were happening at home like the yelling and how my stomach hurting all of the time, and what May would do when my stomach would hurt, she would then assure mc that nothing like that would never go on in their house. I felt so protected with her, my foster mother. She had made me feel special, and I wanted those feelings, feelings that I just did not get at home.

My foster mother asked me if I would like to call her mother because her first name was a little hard to remember I agreed, as did my sister Brenda. I remember watching my foster parents hold hands and watch TV, never once did the yell. I always saw a soft smile on their faces. The couple worked as one, that is what a family is all about I was told by my foster mother.

We would have a TV in our bedroom so we could watch children shows as they both were really into sports games at that time, and I found them boring, and would fall asleep. When sports was on TV we would all sit in the living room as a family I remember my foster mother always asking if we needed anything, she had and a very caring heart. I started asking her the same, she would always say no, but I wanted to show her that I cared for her as much as she did for me. No yelling, no threats of being spanked, no worries.

I started the first grade in September and my foster mother would drive me to school everyday I made a lot of new friends at a new school about ten miles away from my old school.

My foster mother would come to my school for teacher's conferences to see how well I was doing in my studies I was doing great in every subject, I could remember her telling me how proud she was of me and how that made me feel.

My foster mother loved all of my drawings, paintings; she just loved anything I did I always wanted to do more, I wanted her to be happy with me maybe then I would be able to stay with her, I would not have to go back and live like I was living.

My foster mother was true to her words she never did anything bad to me and if my stomach hurt which was rare, I was given medicine to make it feel better, no enemas ever. Aspirin was place in my mouth, nowhere else.

Living care free and happy, no torment, or abuse, no feelings of being unloved. I actually felt happy for myself as well as for my sister.

I was in the home for about seven months before I heard from May (my birth mother) it was my birthday. I had told my foster mother about previous birthdays I had at home and my foster mother had a party for me, a real birthday party with present's cake and friends from school I received clothes, toys, shoes, and much, much more.

I am **seven years old** and my foster mother had made me feel so special and I was told how I deserved that special day the cake had seven candles, as I blew out each candle you must know the wish that I had made.

I wanted to live a happy life, and each of the other candles were for my brothers and sisters, and the last one was for my foster parents. I love them and want them to keep me. As we all know some wishes just don't come true.

May had showed up on my birthday with a gift a new bike with high handlebars and a banana seat she has never done that before, I mean gave me a gift for my birthday that I can remember.

It felt like May was trying to buy me or she was just pretending to care about me, Maybe she did what she did so I would want to come home I really did not know what to think.

I called my foster mother over calling her mother to see my bike; she said that the bike was very nice, May then reminded me that she was my mother and that I only have one mother and to call this woman that was taking care of Brenda and me by her first name.

I was so confused why couldn't I have two moms, I have a good mother and an evil one, my foster mother is so nice I am sure that she did not have to be she but she was I didn't ask to come here I was sent here by May.

I felt like I was thrown away discarded like garbage and someone came along and took me out of the garbage, and told me that I was worth something in this world and that was my foster mother.

May had told me that when school was out for the summer I was coming home and I asked, was Grandpa still there and May said yes but things would be different and not to worry, all of this to think about and fill my mind on my birthday my stomach started to hurt me, I had told my foster mother about the pain and she had given me something oral to make it better.

Well, I want to stay here I thought to myself my second mother is very kind as was her husband, which I really found it very hard to call him dad because I already had one. I did not have the same feelings about my real mother.

Why would I want to leave this happy home? We were now eating better, I have friends, and my sister and I are cared for much better than we were at home, the only reason I would want to go home is to be with my other brothers and sister.

My foster mother had asked me if I wanted to go home I did not answer her instead I asked her if she could get my other brothers and sister? She said that she would try very hard, now I worried about leaving a happy home to go back to what?

It was now June and school was out closer and closer to going home I wanted to stay my stomach was starting to hurt me again, the medicine was not working for me that my foster mother was giving me my stomach just felt like it was in knots.

Later on in the month my foster mother said that she could not help me she gone to court she told me, and this situation was only temporary I wish you could stay but you can't, she had told me how much she would miss my little sister and me she seemed to be sad for me as well as for herself, she called me her bright little girl.

May was back in the middle of June to get us I cried, as did my foster mother instantly my stomach started hurting me again.

I was now to never see my foster mother ever again I felt brokenhearted and pain this just wasn't real it couldn't be I thought about my foster mother all of the time even after I went home, I often think about what would of happen if I could have stayed.

It was time to go home I was unable to have any emotions or thoughts when I saw May I did not know what the situation was going to be like going home. I would be now leaving my friends behind again, never to see them again either, a sad confusing time for me.

Arlene D. Arnold

Home again

My sister Brenda and I were in the car pulling into the driveway of the two-story home we were in before we were placed into the foster home, May did not say much on the drive home like I would imagine a parent saying. Oh, I miss you and I hope we never have to be separated again, or even I am happy to see you, my life has been terrible without you.

Just any words of care would have worked just so I knew that May had care, care as much as my foster mother did as she cried as we were leaving her home reminding me so much of my father standing and crying. I waited for something but she said nothing not a word all the way home.

We were in the driveway the car had come to a stop May had opened her car door and preceded to get out as we followed without be prompted to through the same car door. May said lets go inside her first words since the drive home I did not know what was in store for my little sister or me, we just followed behind May.

We came in through the back door and through the kitchen just like before when we first arrive to this home the kitchen was still the same, as was the living room.

May said to us your grandfather is not here your grandmother took ill after you were place in the foster home and grandpa spends a lot of time at the hospital these days.

Let me show you your room May would say as we followed her up the stairs to the left your bedroom, I almost felt like I was being shown to a motel room there was just no feeling behind anything May was telling us, it was almost like she was being made to watch us and we just were not her children.

In our bedroom I had noticed the walls were different purple flowered wallpaper with a white background three twin beds with fancy wooden frames, curtains, purple plaid that matched the bed spreads, I thought to myself wow what a big difference, maybe this will work after all.

My brother's bedroom was downstairs made up just like ours without the flowered wallpaper.

A few days had past now all of my brothers and baby sister were now home I missed them so much, in the foster home I thought about them and I would get sad well, I am not sad any more now that we are together.

The year was 1968 it was summer everyone was home and playing like nothing ever had happened grandpa was not around, or we did not see him anyway.

The only thing that would complete this family is our dad that was not going to happen I sure did miss him, wondered how he was doing and did he miss me like I missed him?

May started telling us when we ask about dad many bad things, she would not be upset when she would talk she would just say the meanest things like, he was no good, he was a bastard, your father was always in trouble with the law and he had other women in his life other than her, he was just a bad person.

This is what we heard for many years to come never believing a word that was spoken by her about my father.

It was towards the end of summer, I started to see my grandpa again, he did not say much of anything to me or my brothers and sisters, he seemed to be sad, he would go to his room and lay down.

I thought to myself, grandpa used to be so mean, the meanness has gone away, it was not that, grandmother was very ill, an incurable liver condition and she would not be leaving the hospital alive.

That was very sad for me, I was never able to get to know her, and I bet she was a great person.

At almost the end of summer, grandmother had passed away. There was a small funeral, I was not there neither was my brothers and sister, just adults.

Grandpa was packing his clothes and little things, he had purchases a home in southern California, he had given May this home we are in to raise us kids, he had no reason to stay, the love of his life was now gone.

Grandpa had left the furnishings also; he left behind all of his memories to start a new life. Upon his departure to start a new life, grandpa had bought May a brand new Mustang, a car that she did not want us in, so later she ha purchased a station wagon.

It was now the end of August and school was to start soon, as before we went to the foster home, we went shopping for school clothes, the only difference was that all of the girl had the same exact dresses to wear, and my brothers had the same pants and shirts. My guess was so everyone would know that we were bothers and sisters.

Arlene D. Arnold

September 1968 first day of school second grade I felt so awkward, I knew and remembered my friends in my second grade class from kindergarten.

How was I going to explain were I was for a whole year? I was told by May not to talk about the past year to anyone why? I would ask myself was it a secret that she gave us up for a year? I was not able to talk about my foster mother either to my schoolmates from last year I was there, I was living a lie now and didn't know why, people should know that I had other people in my life people that cared about me and me about them.

Well any way I would just tell my old friends when they asked I was not allowed to talk about it where I was and eventually they stopped asking. Just another memory that would be destroyed that was a beautiful section of my life, now I had a father and a foster mother they just did not exist not in my house. Not only did they not exist about twenty classmates from my last school year didn't either.

I was dreaming I just had to be and just not able to wake myself up this is what my life began to feel like to me just unreal.

A gentleman caller for May

Around December 1968 was the year May had a gentleman caller he was from New South Wales, Australia that is closest to Brisbane, Australia. His name was Gary; Gary was stationed at Moffett Field Naval Base in Sunnyvale, California. Moffett Field is about 25 miles south of San Francisco. Moffett Field was closed as a military base on July 1, 1994.

Gary really seemed to love children he had a soft smiled all of the time and I thought him to be a very soft and gentle person, I don't know how May and Gary meant but they seemed to have known each other very well.

They would kiss and Gary was welcomed into the house. They must of meant while were in the foster home, we were all introduced to Gary whom looked like a movie star with light brown hair and blue eyes, a great Aussie accent and build.

May seemed to be very happy in this relationship with Gary she seemed to be at peace with herself not angry, not yelling, and just very calm it was kind of like some motherly instinct was coming back to her.

I remember going to Santa's village, were we had so much fun many rides, cotton candy, feeding the animals and hats from the park.

We seen Gary a few more times, he would come for dinner in uniform, a always a gentleman.

We would go to Half Moon Bay, four miles of broad, sandy beaches which was picturesque in its setting we would go for picnicking and just beach fun.

Or there were many great restaurants there as well which we would go to on several occasions because Gary really loved being close to the ocean as did we as children.

Another great place we would always seem to be was Santa Cruz beach boardwalk in Santa Cruz CA. The best place to go for fun and amusement, they had a great roller coasters at the time I was there as a child.

I remember May being sad Gary's tour of duty was now over and he had told May that he had no one special back at home where he was from, he asked if he could bring us back and be his family and her his wife. She declined the offer to go to Australia to live with Gary but wrote him all of the time; he even called on the phone many times.

After a few months had gone by I did not hear about Gary any more May would not even speak of his name she said that it upset her too much to talk about him, I will never forget Gary as he did make an impression on my life as a nice man unbeknown to me what was to lie ahead.

May seemed to be numb very quiet having not much of anything to say for a few months after Gary stopped calling and writing to her,

My feelings were that maybe May knew that she had made a mistake and she would regret it for the rest of her life.

Third Grade

I was now in the third grade I had somewhat of a peaceful time I would take violin lessons in school, I chose the violin because it makes such peaceful music; I also had taken cello lessons, but went back to the violin.

I really wanted to play the interment for the rest of my life, I would go home and after my chores were done I would play hearing the soft sounds of the strings.

I would play in our school concerts also and one concert I remember was at Christmas time the strings section of our school band was able to play so many Christmas beautiful songs. Can you remember what Mozart's shirts looked like they were white with frilly fringe down the front with fancy fringe at the end of his sleeves, well anyway that is what my blouse looked like also I wore a black crushed velvet skirt with black leather shoes which I only wore at concerts.

The biggest thing I really thought that was amazing that I did was traveling from school to school playing for children and their parents, at no time was I afraid that I would mess up because I knew each and every song by heart I was so proud of myself, After the third grade my lessons had stopped.

At school in October we also would have a Halloween carnival and many other carnivals throughout the year, but the Halloween carnival was my favorite I was a hula dancer wearing a grass skirt and top to match. This was a chance also for the parents to get to know each other unfortunately this would be the first and last year that we as a family would attend any school functions like this, which this function was held every year.

March First

It is now March first my birthday I had a small party at school with my classroom friends. I came home from school and there was a birthday party with my brother and sisters the only thing different was we were not just celebrating my birthday we were celebrating Michael's birthday also. We were born in the same month his birthday is on March seventeenth Saint Michael's Day. I remember asking to have some friends over from school for the party that was, forbidden no reason was ever given just no, never.

We had a quarter sheet cake to share my name in the upper left with candles and

Michael's name in the lower right with candles also, I had no problem sharing my day with my brother I love him very much and would do anything for him. Our gifts were even the same portable radios and other small toys. Our birthdays were together until were no longer living at home and this year my birthday was not forgotten.

I *am eight years old* now not much has changed in our lives except when we go to bed at seven thirty every night May tells us to stay in bed she has to go out I try my best to stay up and wait for her to come home but I always fall asleep, she is there in the morning to wake us up for school. This goes on until school is out in June I wonder to myself where is she going what is going on are we leaving again so many thoughts my head is spinning. It was around the fifteenth of June the answers to all of my questions were about to be revealed.

I was explained to by May there is a very nice person that I want you and your brothers to meet I thought to myself, this must be a very important person for May to wear very nice clothes as ours were laid out also to wear.

It was about five in the afternoon our hair was getting combed and brushed we had already bathed now for the new clothes that we would only were for school were put on. At six in the evening we were in the car driving being prompted by May that we better be on you best behavior or else, I thought to myself that means we'll be spanked, which at that time didn't happen much.

We arrived at this town home in Palo Alto, California. We were asked to get out of the car and we followed May to the front door of someone's home.

A man answered the door. Hello, come in, once again May seemed to know this person very well, they kissed and hugged as we were coming into his home.

This man stood about five eight or nine has very light skin like my grandpa and blue eyes with very short black hair a crew cut. He was very well dressed black slacks and a white shirt he as well seemed to like kids.

His name is Jay we played for a while with him then sat at the table and had pizza and then played a little more then went home.

After we arrived at home we were asked if we liked Jay everyone said yes including me and then May went on to say that Jay had asked her to be his wife you are going to have a new dad. I really did not want a new dad I was thinking to myself I have not seen my real dad in such a long time maybe he has forgotten me I was hoping that was not the case.

My stomach would now start hurting again I told by May lets head into the bathroom towels were placed on the floor my panties were taken off and I was asked to lie down on my back.

May had a syringe similar to the one she had used when I was younger a sink of warm water with soapy bubbles in it, Lubricant placed on the end and placed inside me time and time again until I thought I was going to pop but I didn't and May kept going, she said just breath and relax until the water started coming out of me.

May would start to get upset and yell at me hold it I would start to cry I was in so much pain my stomach was so tight I thought I was going to throw up, she finally stopped and let me go to the bathroom. I was so afraid to say I did not feel well after that because the same thing would happen again and again.

I thought to myself this must happen to everyone that has a stomachache in our home I thought that this was normal and never questioned anything she did. I really never talked about these this to anyone nor did not want to get in trouble for talking about it. I could not begin to think what would happen to me next, it is now June and school is out for the summer.

First Summer Vacation

May and Jay were married during the summer when school was out and a week later Jay moved in we were instructed by May to call Jay our new stepfather dad, I did not feel right calling him that I have a dad Jay gave us the option to call him Jay, or dad, I called him Jay, as did my older brother Brad, and my younger brother Michael.

May would look at me and the other two older children like we had done something wrong every time we would say Jay's name I felt bad that I was unable to call Jay dad, or father I just could not bring myself to say those words to someone that was not my real father. The three younger children, Brenda, David, and Annie called him dad they really had no memory of our real dad they were just to young to remember him.

We had the whole summer to get to know Jay his likes and dislikes he seemed to be very nice by saying nice he didn't yell or raise his voice once.

It was Jay's idea that we take a summer vacation together as a family goes somewhere we had never gone before that was Tijuana, Mexico, a little info for you.

TIJUANA, MEXICO

TIJUANA is the largest city in Baja. Tijuana is best viewed from above to see the entire city and it's beautiful views along with the coastline. There are great beauty hill terrains as well.

Tijuana is a very compact city north of the border. Most visitors who cross the boarder will not see the entire city, as the will stick to the main roads, as not to get lost. Tourist with guides will explore the entire city, and absorb everything Tijuana and Baja has to offer. 12% of Tijuana economy comes from Tourism. Tijuana is famous for it's on the street shopping, continuous blocks of shopping, as well other activities such as greyhound racing, bullfighting, and restaurants for an evening of fun which last long into the night, and into the early morning.

(For more information on Tijuana, Mexico, go to you local library.)

My first summer vacation with the family started at the beginning of July we went to Tijuana Mexico we drove there in Jay's blue station wagon three seats, three kids in the back seat three kids in the middle seat and the adults in the front seat.

We left at six in the morning and arrive in Tijuana early evening a very long trip for six kids to sit still and remain quiet we would listen to music on the car radio, when bored we'd fell asleep. Coming into Tijuana we had tacos at a roadside stand the woman was there with her son he was about twelve years old, they both could not make the tacos fast enough we were hungry and the tacos were delicious we were at the stand for about one hour.

We then picked out a motel room for the night I remember it was so hot there, were cots brought into the room because there were not enough beds totaling three full beds and two cots we then went swimming.

The pool was located right in front of out motel room about three steps away May stayed in the room to watch TV and stay with the youngest sister Annie whom was sleeping.

In the pool we were playing with Jay he was tossing us in the air and we were hitting the water just having so much fun, a while later everyone was swimming on there own but me I was kind of tired and was sitting on the stairs in the water watching my brothers and sister have fun.

Jay swam over to me asked what was the matter I said nothing he sat on the stairs next to me and picked me up and put me in the center of his legs and started rubbing my arms, then my chest then my legs I never thought anything of it I just thought he was being nice.

He would then toss me up in the air and I would fall into the water making big splashes time and time again which was a lot of fun.

Jay had asked me to climb on his back and wrap my arms and legs around him very tight I did as we dove under the water, we swam under and above water for about fifteen minutes I liked it very much.

I was receiving all of the attention for that short time I was second to the oldest I didn't feel like I received any attention at all and now I was for at least for a few minutes anyway.

We went inside washed up took showers and went to bed I went to sleep quickly.

We stayed in Tijuana, Mexico over night and we were awakened by May very early in the morning about five am to get ready to go, it seemed to take a little time to get everyone up and eating breakfast we had cereal with milk and sugar. The car was loaded up and then we piled in I asked where are we going and Jay said for another long drive we drove in to Phoenix, Arizona.

Here is a little info of Phoenix, Arizona

Phoenix

In 1874, Ulysses S. Grant issued a patent for the site of Phoenix and the city was officially incorporated on Feb. 15, 1881. Phoenix had been surveyed and lots were established within the 96 blocks of the town site.

A resident of Arizona by the name of Darrell Duppa had suggested that they name the town "Phoenix" after the Phoenix Bird of Egyptian legend – And the town was named. Arizona gained its statehood with the approval of President William Howard Taft on February 14, 1912. In the1940s Phoenix had became the home to Luke Field, Williams Field, Falcon Field, and the opening of Sky Harbor Airport and for home there would be air conditioning. Businesses flourished, as did tourism, due to the warm climate and healthy environment. The population has grown and continues to grow rapidly, making Phoenix the 7th largest in the United States.

(For more info on Phoenix, Arizona visit you local library)

It was even hotter there I felt sleepy and so hot just like Mexico and we drank a lot of ice water.

We pulled into a motel, which almost looked like the one in Mexico we went to our room put on our swimsuits and then went swimming with Jay, May was outside sitting in a pool chair watching for a while and then went in my little sister went in with her.

My guess was it too hot for her it must have been a hundred and seven degrees at least, May would not swim with us she did not like the water.

The sun was going down it was still hot we were still in the pool swimming and playing, Jay seemed to never do anything until May was not around such as holding me grabbing me and rubbing me.

My other brothers and sister were playing in the water not really paying Jay any attention, no one else was around me when I was picked up by Jay in the pool.

I was asked to face him and he made me wrap my legs around him as one of his hands was under the water rubbing my private area.

He would pull my suit bottom over to one side I would feel his fingers rubbing me and I almost thought he was trying to tickling me, he would laugh as he was doing this to me and telling me to laugh be cause it was suppose to be funny. Jay had asked me to put my hand inside his swimsuit bottoms and rub him also his penis was very hard it felt like a hard pole to me under the water.

I did not understand what I was doing but it made Jay moan and the he would stop he would tell me to take my hand out of his suit and he would toss me up in the air I would fall into the water making a big splash. Then Jay would go and play with my other brothers and sister splashing them with water just having fun.

May had walked out with my little sister they were going to go and pick up something to eat Jay said that was great he would watch us kids.

May was now gone and Jay would returned to me and start what he was doing earlier his hands in my pants again rubbing between my legs.

I thought at the time this was normal I did not know any different I did feel I had a lot of attention like I was the special one, the one Jay liked the most out of all of my brothers and sisters and then I thought I can't even say that because I did not know if he did that to anyone else.

I never saw him hold any of my other brothers and sisters like he held me is this being done to any one else or was it just me just me, I didn't know how I was suppose to feel was I suppose to like this, Jay's hands rubbing me is this love what was happening to me is this part of growing up?

We were in Arizona for five more days the same thing was taking place in the pool daily, only in the pool, only in the evening.

Jay touching rubbing my private area and holding me very tight like he did not want to ever let go I noticed I was getting very sore, but I never said a word I thought I was suppose to feel that way.

We toured parts of northern Arizona, the Grand Canyon, and small places on the way but came back to the same motel.

It was now time to go home I think I had fun I didn't know if this is what fun was, some things we did as a family were fun but Jay was confusing me why did he choose me? What was he doing?

Now for the long drive home I remember falling asleep and awaking up many times before we would finally be home, I was so happy to be out of the car and able to run around as were the rest of my brothers and sisters.

The next day Jay went to work and we were signed up for swimming school at Burgess Park, in Menlo Park, CA.

There would be classes for the rest of the summer everyday except on the weekend, which the weekend was public swimming. I was able to be around other children also other adults this was a great place. Here is a diagram of what it looks like now. Our dentist was right across the street.

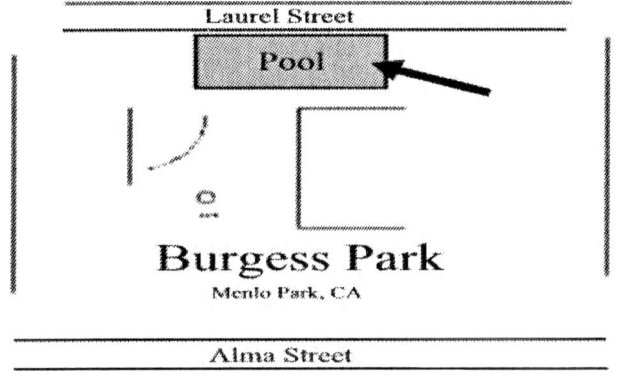

Summer was almost over and Jay had not touched me so far things were okay, it is now the new school year and as usual we would shop for clothes still dressing the same. Now in the third grade and I still have the same friends that is what was great about going to school I felt like I had an extended family.

My classmates were very friendly and I was starting to be asked to slumber parties birthday parties and just to come over and play, that was great and two months into to the New Year I was asked to four parties, and new things started happening to me at home.

Again my stomach started hurting I look back at that time and I was just excited to be asked by my friends to come over, but again I had to have the enemas from May the same way as before and at that time I had a doctor but he was never called May said she could relieve the pain herself.

In the bathroom sink the stopper was put in and the sink filled with warm water and a bar of soap was placed in the water, May would whisk the soap around until the water was soapy, then she would use a cup to pour the soapy water into an enema bag which was red.

She would then lubricate the tip and make me lie on a towel on the floor placing the tip deep inside me; I could feel the warm water going

Inside me, and my stomach blowing up like a balloon she did not stop until the bag was almost empty and again I was in more pain then when she had started.

I was made to lie there for almost a half an hour before I could go to the bathroom, may saying constantly hold the water in just hold it in.

I was in so much pain and misery until May said go to the bathroom, before I was allowed to go she would sit on the toilet seat and watch me moan and groan almost like it was giving her pleasure.

May the told me that she would be doing this once a week to clean me out so my stomach would not hut me any more I can recall this was the time I would also start vomiting in my sleep, waking up gasping for air this would go on for all of the years living at home.

I never understood that either May would just say my stomach was upset that would be my answer, and maybe if she felt like it she would give me some medication to help me from vomiting.

How scary it is for a child to wake up throat burning and not being able to breath.

The next day I woke up and my bed was wet I had wet myself and didn't know why and now this was an every day thing I would wake up wet. Still I had to have the enemas every week the same pain of being filled up with water and having to hold it longer every time.

I can remember holding in the soapy water for about two hours which sometimes May would use dish washing liquid or just make the water soapy with bar soap I remember it burning every time.

Now I was going to the doctor for bed wetting the doctors could find nothing wrong with me except chronic bladder infections I went through many blood test, x-rays, seen many urologist I can remember when a doctor thought I had a tumor and put his finger in my anal cavity, which was very painful.

May sat in the room and watched at that time I was thinking to myself, I did not know what felt worse the enemas that May was giving me or this doctor and his finger inside me I now thought this was a normal way of life.

I was now at Stanford University once a week lying on a bed having my private area washed by a nurse and urine being extracted from me, I felt the doctors were just like May only I didn't go through so much pain at the hospital as I did when I was at home having warm soapy water put inside me.

The doctors never asked me any questions everything was asked to May. I use to wonder to myself this was happening to my friends at school, I thought yes probably so, this is part of growing up this is all natural. I told my self that and never asked my friends at school because it would be too private to talk about.

As I was done at the doctors office May never asked how I felt I guess she could see I

84

felt feverish and just not well, almost wanting to throw up why, at the hospital I was made to drink a lot a liquid so that I would have to go to the bathroom.

May took my temperature rectally when we returned home I was bought upstairs to her bedroom and ask to lay on my stomach just like at the hospital, May would put Lubricant on a thermometer and put it in my rectum she would sit and watch a segment on TV and when it came to commercial she would take the thermometer out of my rectum and read it to me.

I would either have a temperature or not if I had a temperature May would take aspirins out of a bottle and one at a time she would place an aspirin in my rectum with her finger, pushing it deep inside me each time she did it twice her finger started to feel like the doctors did when he put his finger inside me.

The aspirin burned I felt like I had to go to the bathroom but once again I was made to lie on the bed for at least an hour before I could go to the bathroom. A few days later back at the doctor then a temperature was taken and maybe even an enema was given I had faced it this was the way of life.

Jay started spanking me with an open hand in the morning if I woke up wet which I did everyday now, before he would spank me he would put his tongue in my mouth and kiss me as he called it, he would say the only reason why he had to spank me is that your mother asked me to do so, he also said that he really loved me and that he did not want to hurt me.

A mattress cover was put on my bed to save the mattress and now Jay started to wake me up before the other kids woke up so he could watch me take a bath every morning.

I was almost nine years old and my breast were starting to develop Jay would sit on the toilet and watch me wash myself and tell me what to wash and how to wash myself, when I didn't do it how he said he would do it for me no wash cloth just soap and his bare hands on my chest and between my legs I was dried off by Jay and allowed to go back to my room to get ready for school, as my brother ad sisters were starting to get up.

Nothing was really fun for me, or joyous.

I remember the first Christmas with Jay my stepfather, there were so many presents under the Christmas tree everyone had at least ten presents I don't really remember being happy, I remember just opening the gifts and putting them in my room not playing with them. I did not feel like I deserved them they just sat there or I let my other brothers and sister play with them.

Christmas was over and about a month had past I had felt very sad I was crying laying there in my bed everyone fast asleep I could not stop crying.

I remember getting up and walking down stairs May and Jay were at the dining room table and I said to them both I do not feel loved I remember that like it was yesterday.

May said to me just go to bed and Jay came over to me picked me up and brought me back upstairs and put me into my bed, he kissed me like he usually did and said he loved me and said go to sleep. The next morning they both acted like nothing ever happened they said nothing to me I was nobody important or that's how I felt.

With everything happening it seems like March has come and gone, I had a small party with my sisters and brother.

I celebrated my birthday with Michael as our birthdays are in the same month I **am nine years old** now I don't really know how to feel, my friends at school are filled with joy always playing they look happy. I was thinking if they were all going through the same things as I was I should be just as happy but I wasn't.

Arlene D. Arnold

I could remember doing so well in school in the first and seconded grade very happy to learn I had a librarian come to my class usually on Thursdays she read children's book to the class about children and in none of them did they ever mention the things that were going on in our home.

I could remember daydreaming about being the child in the books that she was reading about that would be my escape from home.

I would now start day dreaming in all of my classes I just could not concentrate on what was going on at any given time, it was vary hard knowing that in just a couple of hours I would be going home from school and what to.

I could remember May being called by my teachers and them

Asking her if there was something wrong with me? On those days I would be scolded when I returned home. I was told if any more teachers called May I would be spanked for that.

Now I could not concentrate on school work I was worried about being spanked when I woke up in the morning, having Jay wash me and kiss me, spank me, May and her enemas, now school.

I felt so sad and there was no help for me who was I going to turn to there was no one, just myself. I had to start to block out the things that hurt me and just go on as well as I could.

Be happy more out going while I was away from home pretend I was a different person, one filled with joy and happiness all of the time, the friends that I had while going to school, I'm sure new or seen right through me as did my teachers. My teachers thought I had a problem all of the time I'm sure they would ask how I was all of the time, especially when I went off into a daydream state that was quite often.

When daydreaming I would go to a field of daisies lay down and watch the butterflies flying around, pretend there was a big castle and I lived there and I was treated like a princess, anything and everything I wanted I received, nothing bad had ever happened to me there.

I saw my friend as little prince and princesses they were always happy, their parents filled their hearts with joy never any sorrow or pain.

I meant several of my friends parents at school as I was asked to sleepovers and birthday parties.

Arlene D. Arnold

Slumber Parties/Pajamas Parties

What are they?

An invitation is usually sent out to celebrate a birthday or just a get together of friends, usually of the same sex, and usually done at elementary school ages, but college age as well.

Sleeping bags are usually bought along with the child, and a few personal belongings, such as a change of clothes, toothbrush, so on and so forth.

Nine years old and asked to a birthday party sleepover, slumber party. May and I went to Macy's to purchase a sterling silver charm bracelet, I thought it would be a little much, but May wanted to show some sort of class. Like she was really rich or something, which she wasn't all? I wanted to buy my friend a toy, something like that.

The other girls that were invited said that they were bringing toys or dolls. Once again I felt like an odd ball, a sterling silver bracelet, it was nice, but not something to play with.

Now for the sleep over, I just wanted to go to the party, have cake and come home. I was so worried about wetting the bed; I was in a trauma state of mind. May said that I was going to spend the night no matter what I said, almost like she wanted me humiliated.

Saturday, I went to the party, I watched Cheryl open the gift from me as did her parents, they looked amazed, did not say much, Cheryl gave me a hug and said how pretty the bracelet was.

I never saw her wear it to school. The party is over and now the dreaded bedtime, what was I going to do. I tied my best to stay up after everyone went to sleep, my eyes closing, I would catch myself and wake up again before I new it I was fast asleep.

It was now morning, everyone was waking up, the first thing I did is feel my pajamas to see if I had wet myself, I was so surprised, I was dry as could be, I felt wonderful and at peace. We dressed for breakfast, went swimming, and then I went home. I always tried to have fun with my friends, but sometime would find it hard to concentrate on the moment.

Arlene D. Arnold

The day after the slumber party

Sunday night bedtime I put on my pajamas went upstairs and said to myself I will not wet my self, I climbed into bed and waited for the rest of my sisters to come in before I turned off the lights like I usually did. That night Jay walked into the room walked over to my bed leaned over and kissed me. He put his tongue into my mouth held me really tight and kept his tongue in my mouth what seem like forever.

He put his hands in my pajama bottoms and proceeded to kiss me and rub the inner part of my vagina putting his fingers inside me as far as they would go, oh what pain I felt I tried to tell him that what he was doing was hurting me; I couldn't because his tongue was deep in my throat. I could remember just squirming around and just trying to pull away from him he would say to me keep doing that.

Jay seemed do want to do this more and more the next day I felt very sore and yes I woke up wet, the wetness of the urine burned me very badly where Jay had rubbed me with his fingers over and over again I was raw.

So the next day not only did I get spanked for May's benefit I was washed by Jay and fondled with in the bathtub I did not know how to feel. I pretended that nothing had happened I went upstairs put on my clothes as everyone was now waking up and just sat on my bed.

My stomach hurt I did not say a word about that to anyone, I new what the out come would be.

I felt like I was a mistake I did not feel loved I did not know that feeling what is love is love pain? Is the pain I endure everyday love I don't know what care or love is, May never says the word on the other hand Jay tells me he loves me all of the time, is this what love is I thought to myself I don't want to feel or be around this when I get older, this is pain.

Monday morning everything still was same as usual woke up wet washed by step dad then school. I could not wait to get to school to see my friends, now they all wanted me to come to their parties I did the same things were bought for them as they were for Cheryl. I felt popular that way, that my friends were getting extravagant gifts, I never did, and I guess I was not worth it.

May making herself popular and now part of the PTA at school, she was now someone in the community and I was used to get her there.

A few weeks before school was to end I meant a girl named Dawn whom looked very sad she came to school in tattered clothing, her dresses had holes, as did her shoes, she would be sitting all by herself at lunchtime I would ask my friends to come over to see her they declined, I did not think that I was better than her I went to her and told her my name and she said her name was Dawn, she would go on to tell me that she had no friends; I told her I would be her friend.

She would cry at school I asked her if she was hurt or in pain she said no she said she could not talk about what was going on. At the end of the school day I asked if I could walk with her and she said okay, Dawn had bruises on her I suspected that she was just like me I could not say anything either.

I stayed with dawn until the school year ended I have never seen Dawn again but at times I see her little sad face in my memories.

Dawn I have never forgotten you I hope that you have survived the ordeal that you were going through and that you are a healthy woman today.

Summer is here.

Summer of 1970

We would now tour all of the missions in California, such as San Juan Capistrano, San Juan Bautista, San José de Guadalupe, San Carlos Borromeo de Carmelo, San Buenaventura, La Purísima de Concepcíon, to name, a few which was the whole summer.

The closer missions we would come home after a day of driving and looking at the Mission. The further ones we would stay in a motel over night go to the mission and come home. May said, that we would be well cultured on the history of the United States, also something to write about in our book reports going back to school.

At the motel rooms the same thing would happen, May inside and Jay in the pool with me and my brother and sisters.

Jay never left me alone touching me all of the time everywhere on my body I felt like his toy to do with as he pleases, In my mind I could say whatever I wanted to without getting in trouble I could look at him to his face and in my mind tell him how much I hated him touching me and to keep his hands off of me and just to get out of my life but I can say anything in my mind.

In reality I could only say that hurts, or just start to cry, and then he would stop. I now new how to make him stop, crying, it worked a lot of the time, but not all of the time.

I desperately wanted Jay to leave our home so bad I remembered when he came to live with us and how I thought that he would make May happy was she? It was hard to tell I did not know what happy was for her.

Summer is now at an end and it was now time for the fourth grade.

A new school year, fourth grade

A New Year, school has started old friends from the previous year and some new friends, school was a sanctuary to me to get away from the hell of being at home I was happy to be back. To try to forget the pain at home pretend there was none until I was there I was asked to sleepovers now and I would have to say no the reason was I did not feel right at my friend's homes, I would have to pretend a lot and I just couldn't do that, be happy. Another reason was my friends would see the welts on my body when I changed into my swimming suit I just could not explain to them what was happening or risk them finding out what Jay was doing to me not for his sake but for mine.

This was the year was Baptized Catholic and went to Sunday school

I really liked Sunday school we had Bible studies made many things and I was allowed to the father many times, never once when the church spoke of sin did they speak of the things that were going on in my home.

May had even invited the Father over to our home many times to show how well we were being brought up he, could never see what was happening to me I really wish that he could have.

I was thinking at that times that maybe the Father could have taken whatever evil was lingering around this family and just push it away but it never happened, the only thing that really happened was May and the Father became good friends.

I do believe there is a God but I believe when I was growing up and would ask him for help God was too busy trying to solve my problems, I would guess that there were more important duties to conquer than mine at the time.

In the Name of the Father, and of the
Son, and of the Holy Ghost. Amen.

We Do Certify:

That, according to the ordinance of Christ
Himself, we did administer to

Arlene Dee?

THE SACRAMENT OF

Holy Baptism

thereby making _____ her _____ a member of Christ,
the Child of God, and an Inheritor of the Kingdom
of Heaven; on the ____ twentieth ____ day of
September ____ in the Year of our Lord,
One Thousand Nine Hundred ____ seventy ____,
in _____ Holy Trinity _____ Church,
_____ Menlo Park _____ in the
Diocese of ____ California ____
(Signed) ____ /s/ John B. Butcher ____

Parents { ____ May ? ____
         ____ Jay ? ____

Sponsors
or   Gladys Sorensen
Witnesses

Date of Birth ____ March 1, 1961 ____
Place of Birth ____ Pittsburg, California ____

I now had a God Mother Mrs. Sorenson
whom I did not get to see her much as she
would come over for tea when I was at school,
she was the Avon lady that had come to see
May for many years.

There was not one person I could talk to and tell my problem to that's what I really wanted I would get a card from her on the holidays though.

The holidays were not special to me no was it supposed to be a time for love and peace and joyous occasions what were those feelings? Yes there were gifts even a Christmas tree Easter baskets candy for Valentines Day but year after year I became less interested in any holiday, it was so fake everyone would be nice for a day and cruel and mean the next I did not get it.

This is also the year we joined the skating Lodge in Palo Alto, Ca. ice-skating lessons.

A place after school to go and get exercise to learn how to ice skate I really wanted to be somebody some day, and I would make people around me proud maybe even one day May just might say that I had made her proud or maybe brag about me or even say that she loved me maybe.

I took ice skating lesions for about one year we were members at

The club for about three years, during that time I past my Alpha, Alpha- teaches forward skating strokes forward crossovers and the snowplow stop, BETA - teaches backward stroking backward crossovers and T stops I passed two classes and was very proud of myself as was my teacher.

May never said she was proud of me or my other brothers and sisters we had to be happy for each other.

At the skating rink I had noticed a few kids from my school a girl named Diana that was one of my classmates she was very good at ice-skating, ice dancing and in everything she did. Her parents were there always cheering her on I could never out do her I thought to myself with everything going on at home, it came to be another choir something I had to do or I was criticized how lousy I was at skating May would say.

She would then start to say I would never amount to anything May's favorite words May would also say her mother had said that she would always have problem with me in the future another one was I wish I never had you. May's words of love were always so encouraging, her words of just wanting me to do my best even though I did try my best at whatever I did.

One day after school had started my stomach pain was worse than ever I could not stand it May thought I was going to die or something, I had a high fever I was taken to the hospital the doctors said I had a bad stomach flu I was thinking it could have or should have been worse then May and Jay would just leave me alone. May did, she stopped giving enemas instead she would give me chocolate x-lax or milk of magnesia or both laxatives I was thinking to myself:

1. I must have bored her and she was not interested in doing those things to me anymore, or
2. She really was scared about what she was doing and had to stop. Jay did not.

I can remember the time I was going to be ten years old and a few days before that Jay had reminded me of my birthday almost every day for a month, I really didn't not seem to care one way or another.

I never felt like I was getting older my mind was the same but physically my body was changing my breast were starting to grow, just a little not enough for a training bra though.

A day before my birthday I had gone to bed early I felt tired I just wanted to go to sleep Jay walked into the room and next to my bed, he said May wanted me to come and check on you.

At that time I was not allowed to ware panties to bed I wore a long nightgown that is all Jay pulled up my nightgown he leaned down and put his mouth on mine, I was chewing gum he made me take it out of my mouth I held it in my hand as he put his tongue in my mouth deep almost gagging me, he put his hand on my vagina then took his hand and spread my legs apart and put his finger in side my vagina I tried to scream it hurt so bad.

Then he put two fingers in me I was crying it didn't work his tongue went deeper as did his fingers, then he stopped he took his fingers out of me and there was blood on them, I was bleeding he went to get some tissue he wiped me off as did he wipe his fingers he then kept the tissue on my vagina until I stopped bleeding.

There was blood on my nightgown which Jay had taken off of me and put another on I never had seen that nightgown again I was told never to say a word or the spankings I was getting with his hands would be with a belt, I did not say anything to anyone.

Once again my birthday came and went I celebrated with my brother Michael he had a happy day, I liked his smile at least he was happy It felt just like another day to me I'm ten, what does being **ten years old** suppose to feel like I look around me and see other kids my age happy and carefree, not pretending a fake happiness they were just happy playing I used to know what playing was when I was three and four years old, was it after those ages you were never to be happy or play anymore?

I forget what is it was like to be a carefree child I really want to know that feeling again not in this lifetime I don't think.

I was always with the family on all occasions never out of the parent's sight except for being at school birthday parties or a sleep

Over, childhood freedom there wasn't any for me not at this time in my life.

Yet another summer vacation was coming up in June school is out for three months what do, as a family we went to Monterey and Carmel CA. to spend most of our vacation time on the beaches there. I mostly just sat on the beach and watched the waves one day at the beach I sat there looking at the waves I stood up and started walking towards the water, closer and closer I came up to the waves as the waves were going out I walked in past the water line.

A wave came up and knocked me down and water came up and over my face I quickly dug my hands into the sand before the next wave came and it did, my hand were freed from the sand by the wave of water and I was being drug out to sea I did not scream I let the wave carry me coughing up water and gasping for air.

I heard yelling and screaming on the beach as my brothers and sisters and Jay were getting closer and closer to me, but my body just froze maybe in my mind I wanted to go and the wave would take me to a better place.

I was looking up into the blue sky and next thing I knew Jay was staring down at me asking if I was okay I said yes as he was carrying me out of the water It was time to go home the vacation only lasted three weeks.

Now it was back home to swimming lessons for the rest of the summer nothing had changed Jay had been still the same person he was touching mi kissing me and whatever else he could do he did.

Home alone without May

May was going to L.A. to visit with her Father he has found someone and was getting married and May would be gone for two weeks, Oh my God I thought to myself there will be nobody her to keep Jay company except me, how was I going to survive this what was going to happen to me now? I dreaded the thoughts I was having what is he going to do to me.

The day came to take May to the airport the day I dreaded I wanted so badly to go somewhere also but where was I going to go since I was instructed by May to help out your dad while I'm gone, I stood there and cried I wanted to be anywhere but at home anywhere I stood and I watched May get on the plane, in my mind I was saying how much she didn't care about me also I was thinking why me why did he choose me.

We returned home and I was allowed to go out and play with my sisters and brothers I really thought Jay was going to keep me in the house while everyone was outside playing, but that was not true what was true is after eating diner my brothers and sister were allowed to watch TV and I was not, I had to go upstairs and get ready for bed.

On the way walking upstairs I said to myself what now I was not tired and I really wanted to watch TV with my brothers and sisters, I started to cry because I felt like I was not being treated like everyone else, I wanted to scream but I couldn't who would listen and why would they.

Well I did as I was told to and put on my nightgown and sit on the edge of my bed and wait.

I decided I wanted to chew gum again it didn't help me last time but knowing that Jay disliked it I would chew the gum in hopes that he would not want to kiss me.

Jay is in the room now looking at me he walks across the room to my bed and kneels down in front of me, he put his fingers in my mouth and takes out the gum I was chewing and dropped into the trash next to my bed.

Oh please I was thinking to myself what now he pushed me back on the bed and laid me down, he said what he was going to do next, Jay said I am going to kiss you because you are so beautiful because you never talk back to me because you smell so good because you're so innocent. I just looked at him I did not say anything I didn't know what to say Jay got up and walked over to the bedroom door he yelled down stair you kids just watch TV I have to talk to your sister about something she did.

My brothers and sisters said okay he then shut the door and locked it as he was walking back, Jay undid his belt he pulled it off his pants and asked me to turn over he then pulled up my nightgown, I was lying on my stomach Jay then folded the belt in half and without saying a word swung the belt about five times hitting my backside very hard, I screamed and cried and yelled several times he didn't care my bottom hurt very badly.

He then stopped and just looked at me and said if you ever say anything about what we have been doing this is what you will get.

Do you understand I replied yes still crying it felt like my bottom was on fire Jay has always swatted me with his hands never the belt.

He then turned me over on to my back leaned down and started to kiss me while he was kissing me he spread my legs apart and started to rub me over and over just like before until I was sore.

Then he put his fingers inside me as deep as they would go it hurt very badly I was still crying, but he did not care he just kept doing the same thing over and over again.

He then placed some kind of lubricant on his fingers again and placed one finger in my bottom and one finger in my vagina he was still kissing me and rubbing himself with his other hand I felt sick and very sore, my stomach hurt very badly as did my Vagina and bottom then he stopped put me under the blankets and said go to sleep.

The next morning I was not hungry I did not want to play with my brothers and sisters I just wanted to be by myself, more and more I felt angry I was angry at May for leaving me here with Jay, I was angry with everyone that didn't notice the change in me even my friends at school.

I was so tired of pretending that I was okay all of the time and yet who would I tell what if I told someone and Jay had found out, I would be dead.

Every night was the same while May was gone I was made to go upstairs change into my nightgown, made to lay on my stomach Jay would hit me with the belt a few times and told never to say anything he would always say it was a reminder every time.

He would proceed to kiss me and rub me until I was raw between my legs when I went to the bathroom, all I could remember is crying the pain was so bad from the urine burning me.

The night before May had returned was the worst same as before I was made to go upstairs put on my nightgown and had to lie on my stomach and recite what I was not going to say, I could remember being hit every time I said something wrong, I tried so hard to give the

Correct answers that he wanted but would get hit again I must have been hit 30 times that night.

I was told to put my head into the pillow so I would not be heard crying by him I was hoping someone heard me but they did not.

I felt so sore and like I was going to be sick it did not matter that night Jay had Lubricant on his finger and the jar right next to him, I did tell Jay before I was made to go upstairs how bad I felt going to the bathroom and how much going to the bathroom burned me.

Jay kissed me as he put his finger deep inside me my vagina and in my behind over and over it felt like I was being ripped apart, crying did not help it seemed to make him more aggressive during this event, while I was crying he would threaten to spank me again I tried so hard to be quiet it was so, so hard.

Going to school every day after each night was very hard to do I would cry, I remember my friends would ask what was wrong I would make up something like I hurt myself on the bars or the swing they never asked again and I really did not want them to.

Now I was not happy at school or at home school because I was suppose to be happy around all of my friends, play and just be a kid home because there was nothing to be happy about just remember the pain.

I was suffering in my classes at school I just could not concentrate on my work the teacher just summed it up, as I was daydreaming all of the time and at times I would forget where I was even who I was.

Scared all of the time about what was going to happen next how was I going to survive what was happening to me?

I would often ask God for help and give him reason to help me but I guess he could not hear me my voice was too low or he just could not read my mind, because I would often ask him in my mind for the help.

Daddy where are you is what I use to say all of the time to my self?

If I were with him this would never happen I cried for him all of the time not understanding why he has not come to see my other or me brothers and sisters why?

I could have told him what was happening to me he would never let it happen again he would protect me I just know that he would.

I could only dream about my real dad his name was forbidden to say ever in our home I always wondered if he was okay and wondered if he thought about us at all.

May was now back she had asked if anything had gone on while she was gone that she should know about, the first thing I thought about was Jay and how I was spanked over and over again I did not say a word things must have gone well I hear no complaints May said, still I said nothing I was just happy she was back Jay would not do that to me again I was so, so wrong.

Arlene D. Arnold

The spankings, whippings, beatings

Some history behind the words above

In the dictionary, spanking is defined as "slapping on the buttocks with a flat object or with the open hand as punishment."

Corporal punishment was designed with the out coming goal in mind, to get an immediate response from the designated recipient of the punishment. There is a variety of spanking utilities used in corporal punishment, they could also be called weapons of sorts, this would include; belts, belt buckles, hairbrushes, paddles, leather straps, switches, coat hangers and two-by-fours, cords, branches, and more.

Corporal punishment also increases the risk of related accidental injuries and occasionally death. Often parents are very angry for one reason or another, something might trigger or be a trigger other than the child, any excuse to inflict some sort of abuse.

In my case as with other family members, a leather strap, a wooden paddle, belt, and

114

extension cords were used. A picnic bench was used to lay us on, and tied down or held down by our own brothers and sisters.

You can't even think of crying, the pain hurts so much.

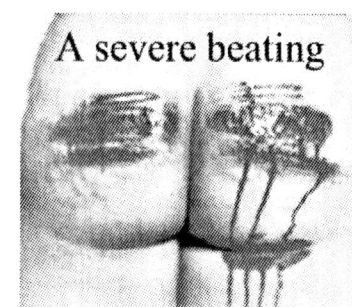

Wooden Paddle   This picture explains itself
*

Leather Strap

* What our backsides would look like after a severe beating.

Arlene D. Arnold

The Spankings, whippings

Jay had asked May to explain to him if any one of us did anything bad she would not have to worry about it he would be dealing out punishments when he came home from work in the evenings, that was around five in the evening everyday during the week.

I tried so hard never to do anything wrong we had chores to do such as dust, sweep, mop, vacuum, and so on when Jay came from work he would check that also, if it was not done right that meant you where going to see him upstairs with the belt I cleaned and did my chores after school but still Jay would see some dirt and I was called upstairs.

The door was shut May never said a word in any ones defense that was the man of the house she would say and what he says goes I was laid on the bed swatted with the belt about three times told not to ask why then Jay kissed me and then rubbed my bottom asking if it hurt, I answered yes as he kept rubbing then told me to get up and go get the next person that was in trouble for something.

He did not touch my private area until it was dark and bedtime or in the morning, before

116

anyone else would get up for now I would still get

Spanked once or twice with his hand for being wet I just thought that Jay just could not wait to wash me in the morning.

Every few days I was called upstairs for not doing one chore or another correct now it had to be correct by Jay's standards not anyone else's my brothers and sister would check each other's chores to see if we could find anything wrong and usually we just could not.

Still it would seem like a chore for Jay to come home to check each and everyone's chores he just had to take out the frustrations of his job on us.

If Jay was not happy when he came home we just new we were in for it I dreaded it the belt really hurt badly, and for what reason he had none to give he just chose names and that was it.

My bothers and sisters and I would hide when he came in the door we became very afraid of him when he called each of our names we would pretend not to hear him, that did not work at all it just made our spankings harder and just a lot worse there was no talking to May about anything.

The bond between a parent and child just was not there May never said anything until it was the end of the day almost the time Jay was to walk in the door, at that she would say you father is here and your chores better be done, May's job during the day was to watch soaps iron and just lounge around never help us with our schoolwork as she was asked many times parenting skills just were not in the cards for her.

We seemed to be invisible just somewhat of a nuisance to her almost a hindrance I feel that it almost bought her joy to here us yelling every time the belt swung down and hit our bare fannies.

Many times my brothers and sister and I would sit there afterwards and talk about how much we hated our parents and just wonder why May bought us home for more hell and abuse, I really felt at that time they were trying to make us hate them.

I believe that we had all been brainwashed in some way or another for whatever reason Jay had given me my reason but I had no reason why or what he was doing to my other brothers and sisters or why?

None of us ever spoke to one another about why they were spanked I was afraid and my guess is they were also what we did speak about was how much we all hate our home and how May was no different than he was for letting him treat us the way he was it was a sad situation for all of us children, we were stuck no help in sight.

Arlene D. Arnold

The Incident of incest between brother and sister

I don't know if Brad had witnessed any of the incidents between Jay and me but he was now starting to do the same things with my younger sister Brenda, Brenda was eight years old at the time of this incident Brad was twelve, Brad was lying in bed with Brenda both were naked and Brad has placed his penis between my sister legs and was rubbing his self up and down against my younger sisters private area.

Jay had come home early I did not know why he usually never came home early unless he had something to do like an appointment, as he walked in the door he yelled who is here? I was upstairs doing my schoolwork I answer because if I didn't I knew I would be in trouble.

My guess is he wanted to see who was at home he new I was May's car was gone, as were my other brothers and sisters I thought as I often came home and no one was there, May would be out shopping or doctor visits or dentist visits, that day I did not know where she was Jay had walked upstairs I still had on

120

my school dress, I really thought that I was in trouble because when I came home from school I was to change into my play clothes and take off my school clothes.

Jay came into my bedroom he asked why I had not changed my clothes I said to him I was changing them right now, Jay said for me to stop and just stand there he would do it he unzipped my dress and told me to put my arms up I did and he pulled the dress over my head, then my slip next I was just standing there in my panties and they were removed also, now I was naked I stood there in the middle of my bedroom cold and shivering I did not know what he was going to do next I now knew better than to cry it did no good.

Jay left the bedroom and then came back with Lubricant on his fingers he asked me to spread my legs I did while he rubbed between my legs he then unzipped his pants, and had me sit on his lap putting himself inside me pulling me up and down on him it was so painful but I was not to say a word just do what I was told.

He finally stopped what he was doing and told me to go take a bath he followed me to the bathroom zipping up his pants the water was running into the tub I was made to get in, Jay had washed my private area and walked out of the bathroom Jay walked around the inside of the house because no one else had answered and that is when he found him or her together Brenda and Brad.

From the bathroom I could here yelling and screaming from Jay Brad, what the hell are you doing with you little sister Brad did not answer I could hear them being hit with a belt, both crying out loudly I washed up and got out of the tub and ran upstairs and put on my at home clothes.

I came downstairs and sat on the last step looking into my brothers bedroom where Brenda and Brad were being spanked by Jay, I felt bad for them both Jay was swinging the belt all over there bodies, he did not care were he was hitting them he just would not stop it seemed like hours but it was only a few minutes I did not know why he was so mad because he was doing the same thing to me.

May had just pulled into the driveway and Jay was still hitting them both I was told to go upstairs to my room I could hear Jay telling May what happed between Brad and Brenda.

She put everything down and said she would take care of it my other brothers and sister were told to sit down on the other side of the dining room table closest to the wall It was then Jay came upstairs and told me if I ever said anything what was going to happen to me he told me to follow him downstairs.

May had Jay hold down my brother Brad as he lay on the dining room table naked May had an extension cord folded twice and wrapped around her hand Jay holding my brother, May would start swing the cord hitting my brother on his legs, back, bottom, and where ever she could my brother screaming in pain.

May did not stop until she left open wounds and welts, blood all over my brother back and legs, and bottom now for my sister no sympathy for her age she was held down and the same happened to her, Jay looked at me and just glared into my eyes I just new I was never to say a word or that is what I would get. Brad and Brenda, were unable to lie on their backs or sit down for a long time they did not go to school for about a week.

May did not want anyone to see what she or Jay had done to Brad or Brenda I was so scared now even more than before was I going to get the same and when I wanted to leave so bad, but were to go what would I do for money I wanted to be anywhere but here. Who was I to call who would believe me, my brother and sister would not say a word about what they had done or what their consequences were for doing what they had done, I was lost in this home of hell yet I was in the center of everything that was going on.

Almost the end of the year

My fifth grade school year coming close to ending which always meant it was nearing my birthday was I looking forward to that day not, I really did not care It really started to be the saddest day of the year for me almost like someone had died, I was sad because on that occasion our birthday party Michael's and mine, and on that day May was happy as was Jay. They both could speak and do nice things only for that one-day almost like I was with a different family for the day.

The day before our birthday party there were spankings for all of us children Jay would do what was now normal for him to do to me, have me in any way he saw fit to have me without me saying a word or even struggling to get away.

Now when Jay touched me I was no longer in my body I would feel like I was on the outside looking on I saw a helpless little girl that had no one to help her anywhere, I could see what Jay was doing to me standing in the middle of my bedroom I could see him pull down his pants and place me on his lap and just shake me up and down.

I looked so limp almost like I was dead I could not explain what was happening to me all I knew is that I was no longer in pain, I was now blocking out everything I was limp in his arms like a rag doll to let him do with me as he wanted I showed no pain I felt no pain and when it was over, I was placed on the bed my private area dried off this would happen now more frequently as Jay kept doing what he wanted.

This experience happened the day before my birthday March first which I turned ***eleven years old*** and many more times afterwards the feeling of just not being there in mind, only in body was saving me I thought.

Even when I was spanked now I no longer felt the pain of being spanked the pain was being blocked out, and I would not cry or show any feelings of emotion It did not matter how many times the belt was swung or hard it hit my bare bottom.

I had no care or want to care I disliked Jay with all my heart and soul God new because after each and every incident I told him, he never spoke back and he never told anyone I still thought at that time he was busy too busy to help me I wanted Jay gone, out of or lives I wanted the pain that was happening to the family by him to be gone.

I would now just start wishing Jay away as many times a day as I could at bedtime when Jay walked into the bedroom and in the morning Jay bathed me.

All of this wishing did not seem to be working then one day coming home from school a month after school had started I came home from May was crying I walked in with David and Michael we just stood there what were we suppose to say, oh mother what is the matter that was just not in our hearts to say.

May finally spoke to us as tears came down her cheeks the first word out of her mouth was it is your fault he has left me!

She sat there and yelled this over and over again as we stood there holding our school books in our hands then May the said for us to get out of her face.

I went upstairs to my bedroom sat on my bed and started to cry was this fault mine did Jay tell her, why did he leave my wish was answered that is what I wanted my hell was now over or so I thought.

I just stayed in my room until I was called I watched the clock it was well after the time Jay was to be home I did not know how to think or act, I felt like a heavy weight was lifted off of me I can remember my brother Michael coming upstairs to get me, it was a bout seven at night and it was dinner time he said with a smile I had not seen that in such along time Michael's smile made me smile.

We sat at the table ate dinner and went to bed for the first time in a long time I was not going to be touched anywhere on my body I could sleep in peace I put on my nightgown and lay on my bed I could not sleep but I was very tired finally my eyes would close I went to sleep and I woke up early waiting just waiting for Jay to come and get me it did not happen.

I sat up on the edge of my bed my sisters started to wake up also my sisters and I went down stairs together, I ran bath water while my sisters ate breakfast.

We dressed for school May was now up she asked if we had eaten we said yes me along with my brothers and sisters left to catch the bus my youngest brother, David stayed behind to wait for his school bus to arrive he went to a special school for the deaf this is the youngest of the boys if you recall earlier I said that he did not cry he was very quiet.

I feel the question being asked yes he was spanked as well as the rest of us whether he new why or not I felt so bad for him as well as my other brothers and sisters did what could I do?

I could now finish out the year in peace I found that I was doing a little better in school and that made me feel a little better, I would now have to hear May yell and scream all of the time about why Jay left she was getting meaner and meaner with time.

Arlene D. Arnold

The Blame

I, as child never did anything to provoke the abuse received from Jay or May nor did my brothers and sisters the severe spankings I would receive from Jay, including the rape, sexual abused by this man I ask why?

Jay told May that he was tired of having to deal with us children, spanking us all of the time because that is what she wanted May wanted to hear the yells and screams of pain, I'm sure Jay wanted to hear this also he did not have to do anything he did not want to.

I could remember her telling us before Jay would come in the door at around five in the evening who was going to get spanked probably there was no reason why it did not really matter, if the chores were done or not my thoughts were that she seen our dad in all of us and when she looked at us we reminded her so much of him for that she hated us which is really what I think.

May said to us that it was our fault that Jay left he could no longer come home to see if our chores had been done after a hard days work, he said that he was unable to relax and that is what he wanted in his life there was never any blame on her part ever. Jay was a mechanic for the Ford dealership in Mountain View CA.

When he came home he smelled of grease and his hands were always dirty he would most of the time not even wash them before touching me, I guess he did not feel the need I was just something there for his pleasure and amusement.

He also told her that it was just not a family atmosphere that he wanted in his life your kids hate me Jay said to her I just couldn't be where I am not wanted.

I do remember my older brother Brad telling Jay that he hated him every time Jay hit him with a belt and Brad said one day I will kill you Brad was now thirteen he would also remind Jay that he was not his father.

Well any way May said that she would leave off where Jay did. She would now be dealing out the punishments. She stated that she would not be so light with the belt as Jay was. We would know and feel every inch of that belt, or extension cord and remember every day what it was like for the hell that we had give her, by Jay just up and leaving.

Sometimes I wished May had an abortion Yes, I would not be here but wouldn't that be better that living in hell I really did start to believe that heaven was a place for peace and when would I get there.

Jay moved to Redwood City CA. about two miles away from us when May had to go out she would ask Jay to come over and watch us he did.

My hell was not over?

As I said earlier my hell was now over or so I thought not by a long shot Jay would come over send everyone but me out to play but me I had to sit on the couch with him while he kissed me and put his hands in my pants, the same as before unzipping his pants so he would not have to take them off, making me put on a dress with no panties. Jay would put his fingers inside my vagina his tongue in my mouth.

I was then made to sit on his lap as he would move me in all directions until he was done, time would go by in which seemed like many hours it was two I was told to go wash myself and to put on what I had on earlier I was then told to go and play with my brothers and sisters I went and sat outside, I could not play and I was in pain when was this going to be over why me I am so helpless, May finally came home and Jay would say to her everything went well he would then leave.

Again I was very sore and it was hard to go to the bathroom it burned very badly I would even cry if the pain would worsen, the pain lasted about three or four days I was just happy he was not staying in our home anymore.

He would be over once or twice a week now while May went out I never knew what May did when she left.

She never took any of us kids with her I really wanted to go with May were ever she was going, I did not care any where but having to stay at home I would ask to go as did some of my brother and sisters the answer was always no.

At the time really did not know the true meaning of the word hate I associated the word hate with dislike like I disliked spaghetti my feelings for Jay was one hundred times stronger than that.

School was out now and we were to spend most of our time over at Jay's Apartment no more swimming lesions, and no more going to church no Sunday school no more ice skating there were no spankings but there was still Jay.

I still went through the sexual abuse which I thought was my destiny we create our own I read that so many times that statement I felt was such a lie I did not want what was happening to me, I thought that statement was so unfair, we were dropped off like cattle everyone was made to go out and swim as soon as we arrived but me.

Helpless like a baby that can't do anything for its self I was undress my small breast fondled with and I was made to touch Jay where he wanted to be touched made to sit on his lap while I was bounced up and down until he was done with me, I was not allowed to wash up nor did he wash me he put on my swimsuit and pulled his suit up from the floor as both feet were already in his swimsuit.

Needless to say I did not have a fun summer vacation there was no more outings or trips on vacations anymore just Jay's apartment almost three months of hell.

My vagina was so sore it just felt like it was ripped apart I hurt everyday every minute of each day I should say It was hard to walk for more than a couple of feet even harder to sit down, I was unable at times to urinate or have a bowel movement I would be sitting in the bathroom at home crying on the toilet seat.

May said I was constipated and once again I was given an enema and Lubricant was rubbed on my vagina because May said it looked red.

A week later I was taken back to the hospital I had a urinary track infection bad enough to stay in bed I was in bed for two days while my brothers and sisters still went to Jay's apartment I was left at home to fend for myself what ever I needed I had to do for myself May was still going out daily.

The doctors did not even look at me even if they had looked at my vagina what would I tell them I could not say a word, that had stuck with me even after Jay moved out I still had to see Jay every day of the summer he was the babysitter.

Two days later I was back at Jay's as he told me he had missed seeing me I did not want to see him the same again would happen all the way until one week before school was to start then it was buying school clothes which took about a week to purchase clothes and shoes.

School was starting soon

May had told us children that she had meant a man that she was asking to move in she had known him for about four months she added for quite some time she would go on to say his name, Wayne. While you were with you step-dad we became good friends and May had asked him to move in.

One week before school was to start I was going to be in the sixth grade this year I would never see him again which was after the last visit Jay was now gone out of my life along with my dignity my life, and my childhood no longer to return to this family, I don't even know if he is still alive nor do I care my only hope was that he did not do what he did to me to another innocent child.

I have lost my virginity at such an early age and could remember every instance of my virginity be taken away from me how was I going to grow up and be a normal young lady be married in a nice white wedding gown have children, and most of all be happy the future had yet to be seen as the past had already been written.

The most difficult thing to overcome after the sexual and physical abuse is the feeling of guilt, if I ever received any emotional or physical pleasure from what was going on.

I never felt any physical or emotional pleasure from the abuse I had to endure, you must get a hold of this truth I was just a child! And as an adult I struggle with shame and confusion, false guilt, and just horrible thoughts of self-worth.

All of which are hard to overcome I fight with my emotions almost daily for those unaware of any type of mental or sexual physical abuse, it is devastating my healing process is still on going.

Back to school

The first day of school was awkward for me how was I supposed to feel after what I had just been through how was I going to act like a carefree child, and not push away the friends that I had grown up with as I had done in the past the friends that gave me sanity and escape from reality?

Wayne did not seem to be interested in children which was a good thing he was an alcoholic I used to hear then argue all of the time when I was in bed drinking constantly never had the glass out of his hand for a minute, Wayne was only in our home for the summer and then he was gone he went home back to San Francisco to live with his mother, I never had the chance to like or dislike him we went to the beach once with Wayne which was the only activity we had with him.

How was I going to bring them back into my life I could not because the damage was already done, old friends had new friends now I was an outcast. I felt banished out of the friendship ring because I was different I don't think what I had been through in the past several years that any of my classmates would begin to understand I was still bounded to silence in my mind I could not talk about my experiences to anyone, I kept the abuse to myself.

Christmas came and went there were not gifts under the tree that year but that was okay for me, not for my brothers and sisters, they just could not understand why.

A few months later in the school year I meant a girl her name was Billie she was new to the school and she seemed so lonely.

I built up the courage one day to go over and say hello Billie smiled and answered back with a hello, Boy I cant tell you how that made me feel to have a friend at school that did not look at me as a use to be friend.

Billie had her own private hell to go through as I did she also had a bed-wetting problem but she was not being abused or she did not say that she was any way, my wetting problem was subsiding it would only happen now when I was having bad dreams about the past.

Billie and I would both overlook the wetting problem we would just play together and try to have fun even if on the inside we were miserable, We started having more friends Lisa who was tall and a little on the heavy side but we did not care what the person, looked like we were building relationships with other people I was even aloud to play after school, I think about three times to go over Billie and Lisa's house Lisa invited the both of us to her birthday swimming party.

Once again I was bought by May to the Stanford shopping mall to purchase a sterling silver charm bracelet I was never aloud to pick out a gift that I would have wanted to buy for a friend, It was always of May's choosing what she wanted for my friend or I would be unable to go to the party. I went to the party watched Lisa as she open the gift watched her eyes sparkle she ran over and gave me the biggest hug and said thank you.

She said I had given the nicest gift of all Lisa made me feel so good about myself at that time in my life even if she didn't mean it Lisa you were so very special.

I wanted a birthday party I wanted to have my friends over for a party the answer was no always I would ask over and over to myself, never did I ask a question twice to May as the consequences would be bad a slap across the face for make her have to talk more than she had to.

I went to school the next day and just made up something like May was ill and unable to throw me a party I didn't tell them the truth which was I was not worth having a party for, that is what I felt.

Understanding my friends always were on my birthday I remember Lisa's mother brought cupcakes and ice cream to the class, I did not think twice Lisa came in with a big box wrapped as did Billie they walked over to me and put the gifts on my desk, we had the cupcakes and ice cream in class I waited until recess to open my gifts.

Lisa had given me a game to play, she said that I could play the game with my brothers and sister also we sat on the green grass and ate our lunch and played the game here at school. Billie said I have something for you also she gave me a box wrapped I unwrapped the box a white-shelled necklace and it was made of abalone It was beautiful the two girls were great they were bringing back my life to me a childhood that I would have if it was not for Jay.

When I came home from school that day my birthday I was now **twelve years old** I thought I would expect a party with my brothers and sisters at least, and May would buy me a gift nothing like that had happened I changed my school clothes and went down stairs.

On the counter in the kitchen was a box of cake mix and pre-made frosting I was to make my own cake for my birthday and I did. I think the cake came out ok my brother Michael wished me a happy birthday and slowly did my other brothers and sisters, I went to do my homework, we ate diner had cake and ice cream at the table and even May finally said happy birthday to me we went to bed and the next day was like nothing ever happened.

I went to school my friends asked me what did I receive for my birthday I made up things I received not to make May look bad in their eyes, in their heart they probably knew that I did not get anything I was sad because I did not receive anything but I didn't show it.

My grades were starting to get much better with the help of my friends, I really did like school my favorite class has always been art I had a great art teacher Mr. Ward I started regaining confidence in myself in his class with painting and drawing.

I can remember when my artwork along with other student was displayed at Stanford University that gave me a great feeling I felt like I was somebody.

I would now draw all of the time at home in my any free time that there was, drawing and painting freed my mind from bad thoughts, when I paint everything is gone for the life of that painting how ever long it takes me.

Other times we spent cleaning the house over and over again, we were not allowed to watch television in our home we had three of them, the only way we would watch television is when May went shopping and as soon as she pulled up the television went off we would pretend we were cleaning the whole time.

School is out for the summer I told my friends that I would be back next year unknowing that I would not be. Summer was here what would we be doing for two and a half months, swimming was taken away from us no more lessons, Sunday school was no longer as was going to church, no television to watch well may had found things for us to do clean pull weeds and clean some more, was that fun, it beats doing nothing I guess.

May was now single and she would always say that the boys were too much for her to handle so, this summer she had called her brother Peter whom lived in San Jose, CA.

May had asked if she could send two children to live with him for a year, it was supposed to be Michael and Brad but instead I was chosen the two oldest children.

I did not want to go to live with someone I hardly even knew I had just made great friends in school I would miss them so much.

I was told as well as Brad to pack our things we would be going to San Jose to live and go to school, I felt so sick I hated the idea but the deal was done. No school clothes were bought for me this coming school year, May said no one knows you there so it would be okay to wear the same clothes I did last year I would go and watch my other brothers and sisters get their clothes though.

I felt once again like I was being thrown away Why didn't May leave us in our foster care our life would have been so much better?

Arlene D. Arnold

My Uncle's Home

San Jose. In California the first civilian settlement was in San Jose in the year 1777. March 27, 1850

San Jose was California's first incorporated city and site of the first state capital. The county is Santa Clara now known as Silicon Valley.

We were now in San Jose, CA. to live with my uncle Pete one month before school was to start so we can now familiarize ourselves with our new surroundings, the house that we are staying in is a much newer one level home, as soon as you come into the house there is a very large living room area.

Walk a little further there I a large kitchen and down the hall there is four bedrooms two on each side and at the end of the hall is a door leading to the back yard, the backyard has two orange trees and in the center of the yard grows many tomatoes in a garden with other vegetables.

Pete is about five foot eight has black-slicked back hair and a black beard, he has May's same skin tone maybe a little darker,

Cammie Pete's wife is on the heavy side, she is about five foot five and she has blonde hair and blue eyes she has a very light pale skin tone.

There are three older children the oldest fifteen years old is Pat, and she has my skin tone about five feet six, very thin with long black hair to her waistline.

Karen her sister one year younger is the same height as Pat, same skin tone a little heavier that Pat with the same length hair hers is long and wavy though.

Chris the son is thirteen has blond hair blue eyes and light skin like his mother he is about five six with a thin build.

I am to stay in the same bedroom with Pat the older cousin we are to share a bed; Brad is to share the bedroom with Chris.

We had the rest of the summer to get to know each other before school was to start in September.

My older cousin Pat had a job cleaning people apartments I would go with her once or twice during the summer.

My other time was spent at home with Karen listening to music and watching television something that was not allowed at home, at that time "happy day's" was just bought to television, which was a great show to watch.

My uncle would come home from work and both him and Cammie would smoke pot, I hated the smell I would watch as the allowed my cousins to smoke it as well, Pat and Karen were both allowed to smoke cigarettes at home, there did not seem to be any rules like there was at home everyone did what they wanted to do.

I can remember waking up one morning still summer vacation the girls were gone as was my uncle and Cammie. Well Chris walked into the bedroom where I was sleeping and pulled off my blankets I woke up startled, he walked over to my side of the bed I was only wearing my panties and a t-shirt he put his hand in my panties and started rubbing my private area. I screamed stop it he kept saying to me over and over again you like it I know that you do, I kicked and hit him until he finally got up and left the bedroom.

He came back in just his underwear and said you know you want it you are just playing hard to get.

He kissed me I hit and kicked him harder now, he grabbed my breast as they were developed more now and I was in a bra, he squeezed the so hard it just made me cry in pain, he left the room before he left he would a call me a bitch and a slut and whatever else he

148

could call me, I stayed away from him after all of that I did not want to be in the same place as him at all.

The girls were boy crazy I wanted nothing to do with boys at all,

When you were sexually abused and you suffered a violent rape or incest your view and experience of your sexuality are affected by what happened to you, I was not ready for any type of involvement sexually or mentally or physical I just wanted to be left alone to be somewhat of a kid, I had missed out on so many joys of being a child.

In September I started the seventh grade at Cabrillo Middle School in Santa Clara, CA. the first day of school was very sad, once again I had to leave behind my schoolmates from a school I should have been at.

This year the choices made for me were just not right at all, I had no control over what was going to happen to me at all I had no say in anything.

Chris was in some of my classes at school he was a troublemaker he would tell boys that I was easy, and that I was a teaser at times all I wanted sex Chris was just a cruel person, school there was not fun for me at all I stayed to myself.

I was on a school break at the end of October I was playing in the sprinklers in the front of the house on the weekend and I fell in a ditch in the front yard and broke my leg in three separate places, just below my knee my calf and my ankle I can remember being in so much pain, I was in the hospital for a day and back at my uncle's home I was in a cast up to my hip unable to move or do much of anything, no one bothered to call May they probably figured that she just would not care, I was in bed unable to get up and do anything, Pat and Karen were taking care of me my cousins.

It was about four weeks later May would show up at her brother's home asking why she was not called, the school had called her and

Said I had not been going to school I was also yelled at and called many names by May for not calling her.

I was in many different casts for about a year went back to school on crutches no one asked why or what happened to me they just did not care, at Christmas time I did not hear from anyone in the family just Brad, my brother who was here with me he had bought me a leather purse I could not use it until I was off my crutches and able to walk on my own.

I n February that is when I suffered abuse by my uncle I never knew he was so mean and hurtful until that day, my cousins and me were painting our fingernail and the nail polish remover was on the top of the television I went to grab the remover and it fell over on the console which was hard wood with a dark stain which was varnished.

Well the nail polish remover fell as I was grabbing it and the varnish and stain slowly started to come off of the console I tried to fix the problem by whipping it off the problem was spreading I was told to stop.

My cousins put the polish on the console and it was my fault for it spilling over they did not get in trouble for it I did by Pete, May's brother came home from work and started yelling, he asked who did it and the girls said I did I was called into the room I came in on my crutches Pete punched me with a closed fist over and over again about ten times.

I fell to the floor on the first hit he bent over and just kept hitting me, my face was so swelled up I could barley see out of both eyes my mouth was swelled up I could not move my jaw to talk, now I have a broken leg and a banged up face the girl bought me back to my room and put me to bed I couldn't even cry I

151

was so dizzy I don't even remember falling asleep.

I was not allowed to go to school and a whole month had past before May would come over to see why, my face was still healing.

There was an argument between May and Pete my things were place into the car I went home Brad stayed until the end of the school year.

My schoolwork was done at home I had many visits to the doctors until my leg was healed.

March had come and gone which is just as well I did not care about my birthday anymore I was now **thirteen years old,** the months had just seemed to roll by, there was not much of anything to do sit and watch television and listen to the radio.

I was gaining weight being in a cast not being able to move around I had now gone up to one hundred and fifty pounds, I knew I was going back to my old school this coming year my friends would not recognize me they would ask so many questions about where I was for a year, I just knew it.

Time went by so slowly I thought it would never be summer vacation I wanted that so bad so I would finally have my brothers and sisters to talk to and I would be out of my leg cast.

June was here and my cast was off but I had to still be on my crutches for another couple of months I was just happy to be up and around my brother and sisters again, Brad was now home also.

My brothers and sisters had so many questions about what happened to me at my uncle's house I told them, then I asked what was going on her since I was gone they told me about another man in May's life and when he was moving into the house, sometime this summer. I said who is he, they would tell me that it was a friend of Pete's the uncle you were just at, my heart fell, what was going on here who is this person what was he going to be like, hopefully not like Jay?

A month had gone by I had time to think, If this knew person would touch me or tries anything I would hit him kick him maybe even bite him, I was ready for him.

Arlene D. Arnold

A new person in May's life

In early August I remember a small white MG pulled into the driveway and out stepped a very tall man, I asked my self how does he fit in that little car, his name was William, he stood about six foot one, he has shoulder length blonde hair and blue eyes with gold wired rimmed glasses, very light skinned and a slender build.

He did not look like he would be someone May would date he looked like a businessman that was coming to sell something, I just did not know until he opened his mouth, he said I am William, where is your May, I directed him by pointing at the back door which leads to the inside of the house he went in.

All I could here is screams by May I am so happy you are here then what are you doing here, then did you meet the kids, what do you think? All questions she would ask to William and they both walked back outside William and May, May said this is William, each one of you, us kids tell William your name and we did and then he told May that he had to go to work he would be back later.

As soon as William left, May would walk over to us and say if you f...ing brats mess this up for me I will kill you! Not what did you think of William, as I thought she was going to say May, constantly thought of one person, herself.

William moved in about a week later I kept my distance for a while I did not say much of any thing to him, I figured if I did not say anything to him our relationship would stay at a distance.

William was at work most of the time or so it would seem, he would leave at ten am and not return until seven thirty pm, long day. He worked in San Mateo, CA, at a HI-FI shop, he specialize and repaired mid and high-end stereos and stereo installations in homes, he would talk about the time he installed a system for Janice Joplin, William did so much more and new so many musicians.

He did not seem like he was going to bother me, one he was never there and two we didn't talk to me much, William had an illness, alcoholism an addiction that is very hard to cure but curable.

Arlene D. Arnold

Alcoholism, what is it?

Alcoholism is a disease, which is treatable with time and patience. For many people with strong character and strong and will, choose not to accept that they are ill, and refuse to admit that they have a disease. These are the people that will not recover from their illness until this person has come to terms with the illness, and wants help, asking for help is the first key to the start of sobriety.

Alcohol caused alcoholism? That is an incorrect statement. For example, does everyone who drinks have the disease? Are they alcoholics? No not by a long shot.

Our society states there is criteria for alcoholism that determines whether or not you are an alcoholic or you are bordering alcoholism. Some identifiable symptoms are lacking of tolerance, blackouts, loss of control, and loss of memory, alcohol dependent.

Naturally produced substances by the brain have been identified as neurotransmitters of thoughts, feelings, and actions and so on. They can identify certain emotional states.

Alcohol metabolism eventual produces salsolinal, which provides a molecule that will fill enkephalin sites and increase feelings of well-being.

On the other hand beer drinkers get a double dose enkephalin, which in addition to alcohol metabolism providing salsolinal because this chemical is naturally present in the fermentation of the hops.

Dopamine functions in the frontal lobe of the brain are associated with reward, pleasure.

As dopamine is depleted, an inadequate neurotransmitter becomes available producing the feeling of which you are lacking in; energy, motivation, no drive at all to do anything, and feels depressed.

When neither there is adequate nor epinephrine is available, a person feels energetic, motivated, and full of joy, or false joy along with many other experiences, this is an arousal of the neurotransmitter.

Serotonin is the brain's emotional stabilizer when adequate serotonin is available.

If someone is depressed and this depression has an aspect of irritability then serotonin is likely low.

Individuals become addicted to compulsive behaviors due to changes in brain.

There is so much more studying and research on this disease a than I have done, for more information on Alcoholism and Alcohol-

Related Problems consult a physician, and with his/her help you will be guided in the right direction.

Also you may want to contact certain recovery groups located worldwide for alcoholism and other addictions.

The first thing you must be identified, recognize that you have a problem and then start on the climb to recovery.

The Ledger

May had said to keep us in line she would start a book this was an accounting ledger, in this book would be all of my brother and sisters names mine included, each person would have at least ten pages with their name on it.

Month												Total
Arlene												
Monday	—	/	/	—	—	/	/	/	/	/	/	40
Tuesday	/	/	/	/	X	/	X	—				45
Wednesday	|	/	|	—	—	/	—	/	/	—	—	22
Thursday	—	—	—	|	|	|	/	—	—	/	/	18
Friday	/	—	—	/	—	/	—	—	—	/	|	21
Start of new Week	If over 100 it was split for 2 days								Weekly Total	146		
Saturday	—	/	—	/	—	X	|	|	|	|	—	24
Sunday	/	—	—	/	—	—	/	—	—	—	/	21

/ Meant Five Hits   X Meant you were to get ten hits

| Meant one hit   — Meant no hits

What a page in the ledger looked like

So now when we were told we had done something bad May would rate how bad the incident was and the number of spankings we would get in her ledger, at the end of the week we would have to bring in a bench from outside and put it in the dining room, our pants were removed as were our underwear and panties, we were now told what we did such as I had made a face at my younger brother, and I would get twenty-five spankings or others were dirty clothes did not get put in the laundry by all of us children or bed was not made before school chores were not done to May's satisfaction, all would be in this ledger.

As I stated earlier we were in line the oldest to the youngest, we were laid down on a bench, May would make two of us children sit on the legs and back of the person that was going to be whipped. May would either have an extension cord or a thick leather belt and as she started, us children were to count how many spankings there were, she would tell us at the beginning if one of us miscounted that person would get the same amount or more which only happen a few times, miscounting that is.

May seemed to love to hear our cries and she never was tired of swinging either, this would go on until May had reached the last person at the end of the line.

William would sometime be there at home and here the cries and yelling and screaming he would just walk outside, this would go on indefinitely, there was no escape just rebellion, one time when we were being whipped and

Brad had lunged out at May after he was whipped, he got up and grabbed the belt and started swinging it at her, did she like what she was doing to he would yell, May yelled get the belt from Brad and no one moved as he struck her with the belt and then ran out of the house, she told William and he said Brad was not welcome back into the house.

It was not his fault; Brad was fifteen years old he was so tired if being hit all of the time, he would actually get somewhere close to three hundred whippings for things I never seen him do, finally Brad was tired of May, he struck back and I thought she deserved every bit

Of what she received I did not want to get the belt, neither did my other brothers and sisters.

Brad slept outside near the railroad tracks and when May was not home he came a picked up some clothes and we gave him some food, May treated everyone like a dog but she treated Brad worse. May would actually whip us sometime until we bled or the welts were so bad we could not go to school, which was often.

The children that were able to go to school were made to bring the note of the person that would not be at school, because she had whipped them too much or left many welts all over their back and legs and they were in too much pain to move.

I remember when may hit the boys and the belt would wrap around and hit their groin area and the girls the belt would come around and hit their breast, did she care no she kept going I remember several times going to school and my chest was sore.

The boys seemed to get is worse than the girls even my younger brother who was deaf, later May would have wooden paddles she would also use along with the extension cord and belt, the paddles had come from a game that she had bought us but never had the chance to play.

At no time did I say I wished I wasn't a girl after seeing what she did to the boys, I really believe that I was stripped of whatever self-respect, self-esteem, pride, emotions, and what ever else she could take from me.

There was nothing left just an empty shell, unknowledgeable of whom I was or what I wanted to be, I was lost, my mind was not my own it was molded into what May wanted me to be, that was nothing.

No hopes for the bright future I would dream about, I remember when my friends would ask what do you want to be when you are older and I would say to them, I did not want to be like May, I had not thought about any professions, I just that I didn't want to be like her.

I am sure till this day May sits back and gloats over her ledger, maybe even relives the times she whipped us because that amused her, maybe she hears our screams in her dreams as there was never any remorse for her actions, none at all.

Arlene D. Arnold

The silver coins are missing

May had collected some rare silver coins and two-dollar bills, I did remember May showing them to use but that was the end of it she had put them away never to spend but to save for a collection that she had started.

The first children she had thought of was the three older children Michael, not the three youngest children, but me and Brad, the youngest would never do anything like that May had stated.

I could remember the day like it was yesterday standing against the wall in the dining room like we were in a firing squad, being drilled about coins that we knew nothing about.

One at a time we were whipped many times as one of us counted and for what I would ask myself, it was now my turn pull down your pants and take off your panties.

Lay flat on the bench May would say as she wrapped the extension cord tightly around her had, I was to get fifty swats with the cord as my older brother just received, May had started she swung the cord and it hit my bottom it stung with pain and May would say that is the first one, do you have anything to say and I said I did not take your coins.

May swung quickly hitting me with the cord ten more times I was squirming and covering my bottom with my hands.

That didn't bother May she hit my hands and what ever got in the way, that was only eleven hits with the cord and May now had told my brothers to sit on me, one on my back and the other on my legs and May said I will ask you one more time before I finish up with you, where are my coins and again I said I did not have them as I was crying and I did not spend them I did not touch them.

May told my brothers to count as she swung and beat me with the cord thirty-nine more times as hard as she could, I was screaming in pain as the cord felt like it was cutting me over and over again I felt sick, and was in very bad pain I was told to get up and put on my clothes.

I was crying and in pain I stood up everything was blurry I found my clothes and put them on, as I was putting them on I could feel all of the welts and see blood forming right under my skin on my bottom and my thighs, It hurt so badly just to cover myself with my clothing, still crying I was told to sit on my other brother's legs while he was asked the same questions and received the same

Arlene D. Arnold

punishment, fifty swings with an extension cord across his bottom and thighs.

The punishment was not over we were now made to stand for the remainder of the night in the dining room not saying a word to each other, we stood there for twelve hours in pain and tired and sleepy while everyone went to bed.

It was morning and we were still standing May had come down stairs and said your younger sister took the coins and she spent them, she instructed us to go get cleaned up and start doing you chores.

May never said she was sorry for beating us as a matter of fact she said that she would deduct the beatings that she had given us the night before from the ledger.

I felt like hitting her so badly but what would that accomplish me getting beat to death.

May would also go on to say that since the youngest sister came forward and told the truth that she would not get whipped for it.

Justice was in the swing of the hand May's cruel way of truth no matter what the consequences were.

This would happen many times not with just the coins but other things that the three youngest children would never do.

I started bonding with my brother Michael

Michael is an explorer he is a kind and gentle person like myself, he as well as I has endured a lot of pain together, out of all of my brothers and sister we are the closest and we could tell each other everything our likes and dislikes.

Michael is a great brother we have struggled together for our sanity after being whipped or spanked as May would like to call it we would compare our wounds, we would both argue over who yelled the loudest or who could hold in there pain the longest.

Michael was in more troubled in school than I was taking out his anger and frustration on anyone or anything that he could, which would often get him in trouble and he would face the paddle at school as well.

But what people did not understand is the way we were being treated at home, what was Michael suppose to do, how was he to release him anger that was caused for him it was not self-induced but, produced for him by May.

Of course she, May be able to never see herself being the cause of anyone's pain, or suffering.

Michael had a paper route that he was doing everyday for some extra money I thought that was great May decided that I would be doing the route with Michael because Michael was rebelling against her a lot for the whipping she would give him, she always said that she would send him away I was hoping that she did not.

Michael was all I had that was close to my age and he kept me sane, Michael would be in fights at school none that he would created but he would finish them, Michael was incorrigible May would tell the school and she never told them why and at twelve years old Michael was placed in juvenile hall.

I had learned Michael's paper route and was delegated to do it I was not asked I was told I had no choice, I really would miss Michael and his friends at school would ask for him I was not allowed to tell where he was, I learned his the route I was doing the route by myself one hundred newspapers, I would deliver half and come back for the rest.

Everything was still the same at home, the ledger was still there and now I had to make a choice at the end of the week either I would get my whippings before the route or after, I did not want any but I chose after so I would be able to sit on my bicycle seat.

The next day I was in pain and still had to deliver the papers and at any time a customer would call and say they did not get their paper, I would have to go and redeliver the paper and five marks would be placed in the ledger book.

Michael was finally back home and the route was split down the middle by May, Michael was upset it was his route anymore I did not want him to be upset with me I offered him my route money, and he said no it was not my fault. We decided to do the route together without May knowing we were given two hours to get the route done, we knew the route would only take an hour so we would go out and talk to the people at Menlo College, which was almost across the street from our home we would watch the students play baseball.

We would just have fun out side of the house we would even go out and get something to eat together.

Michael my younger brother by one year was allowed join the Boy Scouts, so pretty much the time we spent on the route was the time we spent together, we were very close and could talk about everything and sometimes on our route we would talk about leaving the house but we would always say to each other where would we go, what would we do, we would usually talk about that at the end of the week when the ledger was pulled out.

The Eighth Grade

The first day of school I was welcomed back by Lisa and Billie; they did not forget me, they were so happy to see me as I was to see them, they had not changed one bit the only one had changed was me, I was heavier. They didn't care and that's what real friends were, they did not look at me differently I was the same person that they had seen a year ago, I told them where I was and what happened to me they were sad but we went on playing and trying to be happy just like before I left.

We walked around the school swung on the swings and ate lunch together, the cafeteria had a name brand food from burger and pizza restaurants brought in, the only thing was the lines were very long and we would either stand in line or bring our own-bagged lunches.

I was not allowed to go over their house anymore because I had a route to do and there was no phone calls allowed, we talked at school as much as possible before it was time to leave school in the afternoon.

Then on to the paper route we did the route but we did not get to keep the money, May would say that we had to by our own clothes and what ever foods we wanted that she did not provide in the home was not at home.

We did get tip money that we did not tell May about that we were able to spend on ourselves though, May started coming with us to collect our route money tips and all we felt like slave to May.

She would beat us make us work and maybe we would be able to go to school if we were not too bruised and battered.

May would now start a new punishment if our chores were not done to her specifications we were not allowed to go to school, May just knew that would hurt that is what we looked forward to every weekday, getting away from this house having some kind of sanity in our lives and that was school, we were trapped like rats in a maze there was no escape I would tell my friends at school I was not sick when the truth was I had to stay at home and clean the house or just stay in my room.

December was here I managed to bring my friends gifts as they did me, at home we fixed the tree really nice even though it did not feel like Christmas, all of us children bought May a gifts in the hopes that she might not be so mean. All of the gifts were place under the tree Christmas day had come and May came down stairs and sat at the table, we handed her the gifts and she opened them all she said that we did not get anything because we were bad the three younger kids cried while Michael and me did not say a word until we went on the paper route.

We said to each other how cruel she was and we asked for some of our route money in advance and went to any store that was open and bought gifts home for our younger brother and sisters.

I wanted out so bad I did not want to live in this home why did she act tat way? Why did she hate the way she did was it that some of us looked like our father, as she said over the years and would say he was not paying any child support.

She would tell us that all of the time but the fact was the she was getting child support from my real father that is a documented fact.

I don't know why or even who May is, I know that she is the deliver of pain, and that she is a liar.

Christmas vacation was now over and it was time to go back and tell my friends how the vacation went I really didn't want to be honest with them but honesty is the best policy I didn't want them to feel sorry for me either.

Well I told them in turn they told their parents, Billie said if anything ever happened to me I could come to her home.

In my thinking at that time was if I were to run away, the consequences would be death, as it was it didn't take much to get marked down in the ledger line up to get whipped.

I would now go home and do my route with Michael, go home do my chores and schoolwork eat diner, wash the dishes and then go to bed.

Every day my friends would ask what happened at home I would tell them I had nothing to hide, I wanted to tell everything but I could not bring myself to tell about Jay, as their parents new everything else what would happen next in my life.

My friends would ask about William does he ever hit you I said no he usually leaves the house when all of that takes place, I would tell them William seems sad to see May do the things that she does to us and he drinks and he gets yelled at as well.

William did have a drinking problem for that May would never leave him alone she seemed to love him but would belittle him every chance she had, we would wake up in the middle of the night to classical music, which could be heard all the way down the street.

"Victory At Sea" Was on of the on going played from William's music list, it didn't bother me as much as it did Michael who was downstairs right next the room where the loud obnoxious music as Michael would call it was being played.

I would hear William at times get very upset for May acting, constantly yelling and screaming at everyone in the house, William was not excluded. I would wonder why he would take such abuse, he was probably wondering the same about us, we had no choice, and he did.

I was not invited to anymore birthday parties do to the fact Billie and Lisa said that they did not want to make any waves, they would know the answer to be no.

We celebrated every ones birthday at school just like last year, ***fourteen years***, wow. We had just as much fun, cupcakes, ice cream, chips, and soda, were bought in by all of the students. I did not need May to come to the school and pretend to be someone that she would never be, a good mother.

At home it was another cake box on the counter to make my own cake, eat diner, I had more fun at school and that is what I will remember. Michael did not care anymore either, it was a game with us, who would feel hurt by her first, or who could show her that she could not hurt us anymore. Michael would out rank me there, he was tough, and she would soon see that.

I never gave her the notice of any party at school. I used some of my tip money from our paper route; I bought everything I needed to bring for and parties for the remainder of the school year.

Things were getting worse at home, William was drinking more, and May was more abusive to everyone. We would be hit harder, and more often.

One day I thought to myself, if I just picked something up and hit her with it, would she kick me out like she had Brad was, who was live with a schoolmate of his.

What would she do, I never found out? I guess I was chicken, or I wanted to live, but sometimes when I think back I really wish I would have. I would have been out of that hell sooner.

Billie and Lisa had informed me that they were graduating from the eighth grade, I had not received my slip yet, I was waiting for mine, and I did not want to do this year again.

I was told I missed so much school, because of being sick, but my grades were okay, was passed on to the ninth grade. We were so happy Lisa was having a graduation party, asked if I could come, we I knew the answer, but it did not hurt to ask any way, no May said.

With some of your paper route money we decided that you and Michael could go on with the eighth grade class to Disneyland and Magic Mountain amusement parks. We looked at May like she was sick, or something. We did not ask any questions, she said that my younger bother and sisters would do our paper route for us.

It is graduation day, I had to wear a tight blue dress, which I did not like, but I did like graduating, that would mean four more years and I would be out of this house. Billie and Lisa both said that they were both going to different schools next year, I was very sad.

We can keep in touch though. I said I guess we can, knowing that this meant we would not see each other again. A week later school was out, we left on a Wednesday, Michael and I, for three days, that would mean we would miss the coming out of the ledger, and we did. We both had a lot of fun, just wondered why she did what she did, letting us go for three days, wow. We never did figure that one out.

Arlene D. Arnold

Summer Vacation 1975

May started leaving us at home alone leaving the oldest in charge, which at the time was I? The week was spent at home doing chores, cleaning everything over and over again, then Michael and I would leave to do our paper routes, talk to the kids over at the college for a while and get something to eat, and then go on with our route, come home fix diner our selves and then go to bed, I was too tired to watch television, which we were allowed to watch what was on at the time, not what we wanted to watch.

The weekend would come up and William and may would leave, stating I was in charge, if something went wrong I was the one to be in trouble, along with the person that had done the wrong, they both left, there was no numbers of where they would be they just left.

Two days later they would return, not giving us a time or a day when, they would just show up this way we were unable to go anywhere or do anything wrong and when we were cleaning the living room we kept hearing this clicking noise, we just did not know what it was we had found out later that it was a reel-to-reel tape recorder, the tape had run out, and we were being taped.

The house was clean when they came home we did nothing wrong. We did state out loud that "The skies are the limit, we are free to do what ever we want now!" We were asked by May, what did "The skies are the limit, we are free to do what ever we want now" meant?

I had nothing to say, nor did anyone else. We were whipped for that reason, and that reason only. Then May would say from now on when we leave, everything that was said in the house would be taped.

Another week had passed the ledger opened we would now be told if we did as were told that and the house was clean, May would not whip us this week, but save the whippings until the following week. They would both leave, May and William together, and would not say when they would return. This time there was a list of what we could eat, and what we could not, that was it, no number how to reach them if something had happened to us, just not what to eat.

We were instructed not to turn on the television until seven at night, and they would know if we did.

Now knowing about the tape recorder we did not say anything in the house. As soon as they would leave, we would go outside on the patio and talk for a few minutes. Go in do some chores, fix something to eat, and take our food outside to the patio. I would say that I felt like I was in a prison camp. We would fold our newspaper and go on our route, leaving the younger children at home. They new not to touch or say anything out loud or they would be heard.

We came back home in about an hour, didn't want to stay gone long time while May and William were gone.

It was about four in the afternoon, we decided that we were going to watch television, but we would plug in headphones so the television was not heard. We would watch without saying a word, at the end of the program and there was a commercial we would pass the headphones to the next person, so everyone had a chance to hear the what was going on, everyone except David, he was deaf.

We would make something for diner, and then go back and watch more television. Why? It was something we were unable to do if May or William were home we had no privileges to watch television, and we found it to be amusing.

After each trip, May and William would seem tired, William would get a beer and sit and listen to his music May would go to bed and the next day William would be bouncy and go to work, May would stay in bed.

I remember the time after one of their outings and William had gone to work, May called all of us children upstairs, we would all stand at the foot of the bed and May would tell us to jump out of her bedroom window, she was wide-awake, and I just stood there looking at her and May yelled again, "I said Jump out of that window" again I just stood there, as did my other brothers and sisters.

Michael said I'll do it he opened up the window walked outside on to the roof and jumped into the bushes, he yelled from the ground don't be afraid you wont hurt your selves.

My younger brothers and sisters were crying I could not believe she was telling us to do that, May then told us to leave her bedroom and close the door we did, we looked at each other like what happened to her, she is a lot crazier.

She would rather see us dead than alive what was going through her mind, was she just pretending to be crazy to see who would jump, she had fallen back to sleep and later when she woke up my younger sisters asked her, why did you want us to jump out of the window? They would ask that question over and over until May answered saying I don't know what you are talking about I would never do anything like that.

I looked at May, as she was a liar I knew she had known exactly what she was doing, what game was she trying to play now?

The summer pretty much was the same, they would leave for a few days, May and William never to know where they were or what they were doing.

I can remember cleaning the house one day, we had decided to clean May and William's bedrooms, picks up the floor, made the bed, and wipe off the nightstands, what ever was spilt on the nightstands had dripped into the drawer.

We opened the drawer half way and there was a baggie filled with green leafy stuff, Michael said, wow that sure is a lot of pot I said drugs he said yes, we had finished cleaning the room closing the nightstand drawer, I walked out of their bedroom and just sat on the top of the stairs I watched everyone walk down stairs as I sat, I thought to my self is this why she treats us the way that she does? I walked down stairs we went outside and talked.

We said that we would pretend that we did not see anything.

This time when May and William came home, we told them that we had cleaned the house including their bedroom. They were upset, but didn't do anything. They both just went upstairs. We did not see them until the next day.

This would also be the year I really started to like the singer "John Denver", to me John was the only musician I would go on to listen to for many years to come, he sang peaceful ballads at that time in my life I need peace, in my mind at least. I would also become a member of John's fan club. He was a special man, reached millions, of hearts, will always be remember in mine.

Arlene D. Arnold

The arguing, screaming, and fighting

May and William would fight all of the time now William would say he was tired and wanted to walk upstairs and go to sleep, May would follow him, pulling and tugging at his clothes.

Doors would slam at all hours of the night May would yell constantly at William, you are nothing but a no good alcoholic, why are you here? Music would blare all night long now.

William would get upset and leave, but would be back in twenty minutes. May was being very abusive to William as well, throwing things at him, throwing things at us. May was just out of control. She would also get in her car and take off; she would only be gone a few minutes.

Were they both on drugs, I would ask myself? We would continue to do the normal chores that we were to do on a daily basis. Pick up thinks that had been broken through the night by May.

I said to my self, "William, you should go before she does something very bad to you." He never did defend himself against May.

When she hit him, he would just block his face. There were scratch marks all over him.

William would start drinking more and just passing out I did not matter how much May would yell at him, he could not hear her,

William was sick, he had an illness, and May just could not see it she was hateful all of the time.

May's new thing to do was to slap if as you were walking by her she would slap you, and the she would say you know why and keep walking, her long fingernail would cross the face of anyone who was in her way at the time leaving open scratch marks across your face if you stood there long enough, you might get two slaps, so as the first slap was coming you had better move quickly.

The ledger was still used it would now be two weeks which meant you received more whippings the same was done the we were made to sit on the person who was to get whipped as May would swing whatever device she had to use on us, we would now be angry and upset with the person who held us down and May, she knew what she was doing, taking away our closeness as brothers and sisters, turning us against each other. I still had Michael, as we would do our routes together.

He never hated me because I had to do what I was told.

With my other brother and sisters the hate and resentment would only last for a few days, they would know that it was not any ones fault but May's. I could remember when we all said we wanted to leave but there was nowhere to go we were stuck, there were no relatives that we wanted to go to and tell what was going on, they were May's brothers and they acted just like her, or even worse to their children

All I wanted was school to start I was loosing my sanity as were my brothers and sisters being stuck in this house day after day, I should say prison camp.

I did not even get to ready my self for high school, which I new was a much bigger experience that elementary school.

We had not gone shopping for school clothes and yet school was starting in two weeks.

I asked May if we were going shopping for school clothes, May said I'd give you one hundred dollars of your paper route money; you can take that and go buy some pants.

She then said the rest of your money is gone, you will have to start paying for food, and the light bill, electric, and so on, anyone who work will do the same.

I was wondering why she had to take money from us, money that we were earning, because we never received any from her. What was she doing with the child support money she was getting? Or the welfare checks that she would receive, it sure was not being spent on us children. Maybe it was for her drug habit, what ever that may have been, because she surely was not normal by any meaning of the word.

Arlene D. Arnold

High School, Freshman Year

A little history of the area before Menlo-
Atherton came to be;

*Menlo-Atherton High School located at 555
Middlefield Rd. Atherton, CA 94027.*

*Menlo-Atherton High has its own history in
the property upon which it was built. Most of
the land in the Atherton area once was part of
the great Pulgas Ranch, owned by the Arguello
family.*

*In the 1860's, Joseph A. Donohoe
purchased the forty-acres of land now
occupied by the high school; a local merchant
who built his home was to be the home of
Joseph A. Donohoe and five generations of
Donohoe family there after. The property was
purchased from the Donohoe family, by the*

My Past Was Written, The Taking of Innocence
school district on May 31, 1949, Menlo-Atherton High School was established in 1951. Opening day was September 24, 1951.

I started my first day of High School in September of 1975 a freshman I saw a lot of new faces a lot of students from Encinal elementary school as well, the first day was just registering for classes and then orientation in the gymnasium, school was from eight in the morning to four in the afternoon, I was scheduled for nine classed. I wanted to take the classes I would need to graduate early Math, English, Science, History, and Physical Education, doubling up on most of them. Who was to know what would take place at home, and I would just have to leave.

I pretty much stayed by myself ate lunch alone would read at lunchtime and do the homework I was suppose to do at home, that way when I went home I would just have my chores and my paper route to do.

One day I had gone home did the route with Michael did the chores ate diner and was getting ready for bed, well this is what too place me along with my younger sister had to get three plate glass mirrors from the bathroom and place them on the floor in the kitchen, we were wonder why we just didn't know what May had up her sleeves now. What was on her mind? We were asked to take off our clothes in the middle of the kitchen floor, now there were three mirrors on the floor and we were asked to choose a mirror and sit down in front of it.

William would walk into the kitchen to get something and would tell May to do what ever she was doing in the bathroom.

He did not stare at us yet shook his head and walked away as William walked into the kitchen and so did my brothers, the youngest David, who is deaf looked at us and then looked at May, he as well shook his head and walked away.

Our naked bodies were there on display for everyone in the house to see how humiliated I felt, as did my sisters. We were not allowed to say a word.

May sat there like an instructor now she would instruct us to spread our legs apart, she then would ask out loud what do to see? One at a time we would have to answer her, then she would instruct us to spread our vagina apart and look at it and to say what we saw, again one at a time we had to explain what we saw.

Then May had us put our hands on our breast as we were all developed by now, she would ask us how that felt we had to explain once again, one at a time how that felt we were then allowed to get up and put on our nightgowns, go into the bathroom and be watch by May as we washed our vaginas.

How she made us feel? Raped by eyes staring at our naked bodies, belittled in any and every way May could break us of any self-esteem we had.

We were then told we were at no time to le anyone touch us there, our vagina, and if we did the price we would have to pay.

That meant no boys around us, not even just friends as she stated. I will check you from time to time also to see if you had let anyone touch you.

At the age of *fourteen,* I had not started my period, my two younger sisters did, and they were nine and ten. I just thought that I wasn't going to have a period for the reason being, what Jay had done to me when I was younger. I was never asked by May either.

That would not be true, two months later I started my period, maybe my body had to catch up, I just don't know.

Arlene D. Arnold

A month into the year I meant a nice guy

One day three months in to the school year I meant a boy his name was Mark, I was at lunch sitting in the front of the school under a tree eating my lunch, which we had forty-five minutes to eat, well I noticed a shadow on the grass a silhouette of someone wearing a hat and I looked up and this person said hello, I answered back with a hello, he asked if he could sit down next to me, I said yes I told him up front that I was not allowed to be around any boys he had asked why? I told him it was May's wishes, and if I did not follow them I would be in a lot of trouble.

He said to me my name is Mark what is yours, I told him, and he said that was a great name, Mark was a senior in high school and my guess was that he wanted some friendship without having a commitment and that was great, because I was not ready for any king of relationship.

Mark was tall and handsome he stood about five eight a slender build, blue eyes and black long wavy hair, black mustache, and a creamy complexion all that and a great personality to boot.

As for May's whishes he would say what is done at school she has to never know, we would talk about him mostly, never about personal life, he was dressed like a cowboy most of the time, including the hat and boots.

He would tell me he was from Livermore CA., which was cowboy country, he chewed tobacco and spit all of the time, but I overlooked that because he was a very nice person.

Mark would wait for me outside my last class of the day and walk me home after school, we would always take a different routes home as to miss May if she was out looking for me.

I told Mark I had a paper route to do after school with my brother, he thought that was great and he wanted to meet my brother, I told him were he could meet us over at the college, and he did. When the two meant they had already known each other through friends, I thought that was great. We did the route together.

The next day was the same Mark would carry my book for me also this was the day May would be driving to the school and sees us walking. She stopped and told me to get in the car, Mark had given me my books and said I will see you tomorrow.

I was driven home and grilled, who is that boy May had ask? I said just a person I meant at School, May said does he touch you? I would say no. What does he want with you? Just to be friends, that is all.

May had asked for his home number she called him and asked the same questions my guess is that he would say the same thing as me, she had asked Mark to come over on Saturday for a picnic outing; my guess was to ask him more questions.

The next day at school he asked me what happened, I told Mark not much of anything, May just wanted to know a lot about you, I said, I don't know why. He said that he would come, just to hear what she had to say.

The ledger was overlooked and Saturday was here, Mark showed up at eleven thirty like he was told.

Lunch was packed and we were taken to the park and May grilled Mark, what do you want with my daughter she would ask? We are just friends at school mark would answer.

May said I hope that is all, she made Mark feel awkward the whole time we were there at the park.

Monday he would tell me how weird she was I told him I know and I was sorry he had to go through that. We would continue to walk home after school until Mark had joined the swim team after school. We would only talk at school now, and I would walk home alone.

Mark would tell me the only reason he was in this area was he was having problems at home with his dad in Livermore, and he was trying to fix the problem between the both of them.

He was living with his mother in Redwood City, until he could go home, they had been divorced since he was ten years old he said he really liked Livermore though.

One day his father had called him and asked him back home, he told me about that and he would be going home at the end of the semester, I was sad that Mark was leaving but happy that he was going home, that is where he wanted to be I never seen or talked to him again. He was a good friend.

The second semester had started I was back under my tree in the front of the school doing my homework, I sat there just thing about Mark, was he happy now, is he getting along with his father. The struggle between father and son at least he was not being beat by his father there was just the struggle to get along with him, as Mark was changing with age. He was no longer a little boy, he was a man, and Mark did not want to be treated like a child anymore.

Well lunch was over and time to go back to class I thought the teachers were great in high school nothing like elementary school. They seemed to make you more independent I liked that.

School was out time for the long walk home by myself, which was okay. I had time to think. What was going to happen today when I arrived home? The reason I asked was it was Friday. I knew the ledger would be there waiting.

I would come in the house go upstairs and change my clothes I did not see anyone when I came in. I looked out back and there was May. I saw the ledger on the table; I kept walking toward the front door, opened it, and went out and sat on the porch to fold my papers. Michael had just walked up, he started folding papers also, we both left on the route.

I asked Michael what do you think you're going to get and he said I don't know, and you I said I don't remember doing anything wrong. Michael then would say well you know how that is it really doesn't matter, the _itch, will always find something I said I know, we were done with the route, went home.

Walked into the door Michael was the first to get it for doing something at school we had hid the belt and the paddle, that did not help, May had an extension cord, we would soon find out that would hurt worse. May seemed to swing that harder. It felt like knives cutting your back and bottom, and we were suppose to be ridding a bike, to do our route?

Michael received sixty swings of the cord it was my turn, I said out loud, I did not do anything, and May would say that is right lately your chores have not been up to par.

I received twenty-five swats with the extension cord when she was done, I had black and blue welts on my backside, oh get this it was my birthday as well, I was told to go in the kitchen to make my cake.

I said I did not want any cake and for what, I would say it isn't my birthday and would May said fine go to your room, and I did for the rest of the night, saying in a low voice how much I hated her and I wished that she would just die, I was **fifteen years old**, and it did not feel like it, at all.

What was I suppose to feel like? I was not happy the only time I am somewhat happy is when I am out of this house. "The House of

Hell", is what I would call it after my birthday had come and gone. The next day was Saturday, I did not come down for breakfast, and I stayed there until it was time for my route. I did the route as usual.

Came home went to my room, listen to music and went to sleep. I had to face I, this was my life until I left home, and I better just try to deal with it.

May would ask where was Mark one day she drove by and I was walking alone on my way home from school I never did tell her he went home to live with his dad, get in the car she would say, she asked again where is Mark? Do you tell him everything even when I whip your ass she would say, I said Mark had left the School; I don't know where he is.

May would say I think you scared him away he had pity for you and he never did like you, she would say ugly things like that now, over and over every day. It was just another from of breaking a person, lowering their self-esteem, I would try overlooking May's verbal act of stupidity.

When I couldn't I would say she was wrong I would get slapped for talking back, there was just no way to win in this situation

I had to get through high school this was? School was not hard my life at home was hard, just living seem to be hard.

I really get to know anyone this year, except Mark, and he was gone. School was out, maybe next year; I will meet someone new at school, maybe.

I did okay as a freshman my grades were okay as well, I looked at it this way at least I made it to finish out the year, I did not mention any holidays, because, the only one who celebrated was May and William, it was not mentioned.

Arlene D. Arnold

Summertime 76'

I did not do much I woke up cleaned the house as did my brothers and sisters, did the route as usual with my brother Michael, I liked staying outside in the back yard, just looking at the trees, looking at the blooms on each and every branch just thinking about what I was going to do when I left home, my thoughts would be who would want me? If I told my story to anyone how would thy take it? How many questions would I have to answer? So many thoughts would always go through my mind.

One day thinking the same thoughts I had a vial of red lipstick in my pocket, which I was not allowed to ware I also had a mirror I sat behind the berry tree in the backyard and just started to cover my entire face with the lipstick, looking in the mirror I saw someone different, I was red faced I thought to myself is this the only way that I could change who I was, who I am? This would never work and it was messy to clean up I never wanted to be myself I always wanted to look like and be someone else but that would never change the

200

inside, my mind and thoughts, why keep trying?

I wanted to be away from the world people, and civilization, I wished on a daily basis that I could be on an island, by myself and never to be humiliated, beat, and most of all never rape, and my soul stripped away from me.

I just exist I don't have a mind of my own and I don't even get to think for myself.

One day I decided to purchase a diary from the local pharmacy in Menlo Park before my route.

I had a friend that I could talk to now some one who would not put me down for anything I did, something that was mine I could tell my thought so, and would be secret.

I started my diary from this month and started going backwards to everything that hurt me in my past, I wrote about everything and one day after my route I had come home and my diary was moved, I thought to myself my sisters must have move it.

I unlocked it and started writing more and more the further I went back and the more pain I would feel, so I decided I would write what was currently happening in my life and then go back on a daily basis.

Summer was almost over but I had written down everything that I could remember, locked in a safe place I moved my diary from my drawer to the top shelve in the closet and I was the only one who had the key.

This summer I notice we were not being whipped anymore or May's arm was just recuperating I don't know she wasn't leaving us at home alone and going away for the weekends anymore either,

Was she changing, I think that she was wrapped up with my brothers in Boy Scouts and with William, the new person in her life.

May did seem to care if we were home at a certain time or not, nor did I want to take advantage of that last remark, there was no telling when she would change or just flip out so my thoughts were why chance it.

This summer I would be able to ride along with the police department, which was a community program for youths in the area to get to know the officers in our community.

I wanted to do this so that maybe one day if I ever had the nerve to tell anyone what was happening in our home I would have confidence built up enough to tell that officer what had happened in our home.

I did the ride along only twice I never really was able to gain confidence to say any thing either, I just knew the officers were very nice, I thought to myself, why screw up their lives with my messy life I was living, it just would not be right, that exactly what I was thinking.

A few weeks before school was to start again I was given some money, money that I had made from our route to go and purchase school clothes, I was happy to buy what I wanted to ware that would not be true either, half of the clothes I bought I was told I could not ware for reasons unknown to me, May never gave any reason I was limited in my clothing to ware to school now I hated my life I wish I could! At that time I didn't even know what I wish I could, I just said it often.

A few days before school I was back thinking and writing every thought into my diary, leaving out not one word spoken to me on a daily basis, or what upset me.

My thoughts on this diary was if something was to ever happen to me, the world would know what kind of life I had lived, by now I just wanted to yell out what everyone had done to me, I just couldn't.

Do you know the feeling of just wanting out of the body that you are in, just being in another place, in another time, that is what I was feeling like, just let me out of the life I was in and place me in another, that is what I would ask GOD all of the time it wasn't working I was here for a reason, that reason was unknown to me.

My Sophomore Year

What was going to happen this year, Only God knew, I pretty much started out the year like I did last year, I would choose the maximum classes, which was nine I really wanted to have the most important classes behind me and that would be Math, English, Physical Education, Science, and History I did decide to take one more class though, and that was Navy R.O.T.C. I was really looking for a future and I thought the Navy seemed like a good future for me.

Well I started out doing my homework as usual under the big oak tree in front of the school at lunchtime, I had noticed a guy and a gal walking by me for the last few weeks without saying anything, I said to myself the next time they walk by me I will say hello, just so they didn't think I was a stuck up kid, or even worse.

The next day I saw them both together as usual I said hello, they both walked up to me and said hello back.

They both had told me they didn't want to say much to me because I seemed wrapped up in my work I said I was but I was able to talk to them as well. I introduced myself as did they Katherine, and D.D., they both would say.

I remember that they both were so easy to talk to, for the remainder of my high school years, both Katherine and D.D. had become my best friends, we would set up classes together at the beginning of each and every semester if we could, the only class I would not give up is R.O.T.C., which was a class I really loved.

In the R.O.T.C. class I had a great commander he was very fatherly and he cared about all of his students, we would tour many ships in Alameda, and San Diego, Naval Base.

This class was designed to provide and make the students knowledgeable in the arts and sciences of Naval Warfare, also established to educate and train qualified young men and women for service.

Katherine, and D.D., really did not share my views on the class, which the class was not for everyone.

Katherine to me looked like a beauty queen, she stood about five foot five or six, She had long black wavy hair, a light cinnamon complexion, brown eyes, and a great figure and well dressed. D.D., which I had found out was Katherine's cousin, stood about five eight or nine and a darker complexion than Katherine's, he had sweet brown eyes, and short black hair, a great build, and well dressed also, two great people.

Both Katherine and D.D. always lifted my spirits when I felt down. I can recall sitting down with Katherine at lunchtime, just her and me when D.D. would be off somewhere else, or doing something else, we would talk. I had finally told someone that I could trust about my life. I would go on to tell Katherine everything, Jay on up and later when I felt more confident, I had told D.D. I did not want them to feel sorry for me, I just wanted friendship, and that is what they gave me. They understood me, and my struggles to be normal, like they were.

I would be so happy to go home and put them in my Diary. My spirits were lifted so high, I felt good, I even started to be happy also, and I felt like somebody.

I was now doing my schoolwork at home after my paper route on a daily basis now I had friends to walk with and talk to.

I remember Katherine would always refer to May as the witch. Katherine would ask did I, did the witch do anything to you today? I would say no. Katherine would ask to call me when I went home from school. I had asked May, and she said okay. Well, one day

Katherine called, and asked to speak with me, may have told me to pick up the phone downstairs, it was Katherine.

Katherine started the conversation did the witch hang up the phone? I said I didn't, I did not hear a click, and she is upstairs, I'm not. Just at that moment, I was told to hang up the phone. May came down stairs and said, what do you tell your friends at school for them to say those things bout me?

I said I just tell them the truth and I was slapped for that answer and told she is no longer to call this house, I had to tell Katherine the next day at school, she said that she was sorry for what she said, but the truth must have hurt, I then told Katherine I was slapped for that also, May's name was no longer a witch; her name would changed to bitch in all the later conversations about her.

My diary is missing

I would write everything in my diary, my life as I had said earlier. I came home after my route one day looked in the closet; on the top shelf my diary was gone. I had asked my sisters if they knew where my diary was, they said no. I sat on my bed and just started to cry, that diary was like a lifeline to me and it was missing.

I went to school the next day and had told Katherine and D.D. that my diary had been taken; the first thing they would say was the bitch took it. They could have used other choice words, but they didn't. I had told the both friends what I wrote in the diary, my thoughts and feelings, my life. I wanted it back. I had written all about the incest, rape, and the beatings, like it was someone else's life, not mine.

My stomach was hurting very badly I was even getting sick at school. Just the thought of someone else reading my diary made me sick.

The weekend had come I did not say much at home I just didn't feel like talking to anyone. I had gone upstairs; once again I had looked for my diary. I looked in my top drawer of the dresser, under my sock and panties, there it was, my life, my diary. It was cut open, the pages ruffled up.

May had walked into my bedroom she would say I did not know what that was, all I would know is it was a book and I opened it and read it. Who's' life is that? May would ask? At that moment, I was glad I had not given anyone a name they were people with numbers. Nothing in my diary seemed to ring a bell to her I guess.

She acted like she was a great parent showing false concerns about the child in the book. I wanted to say to her, your looking at her, but I could not bring myself to say those words.

Everything I mentioned in my diary was mostly about her and my stepfather Jay and how could she not know? I told her that I was holding the diary for a friend. She did not say anything else. At that time in my life, I was so happy I did not use names, for some reason, I was smart; this could had been any ones diary.

On the other hand I hated May for invading my privacy reading my thoughts, and she did not even have a clue, a clue of what she had done, done to my life.

My diary would now be placed into my backpack and taken to school I would leave it

My Past Was Written, The Taking of Innocence
in my locker, At lunchtime I would make the time to write in it, or after school I never bought my book of thoughts home again.

Arlene D. Arnold
The date from hell

I was in science class, which I had taken with Katherine and D.D. In this class there was a guy named Lindsey he seemed to be interested in me, I had asked Katherine and D.D. what they had thought about him they said he seemed like a nice person.

Lindsey was a junior in high school and on the football team about six-feet tall, blonde hair, blue eyes, very good looking, and well dressed. Knowing my past as they both did, Katherine and D.D. both said I should try going on a date, well Lindsey had asked me out on a date I told him I would have to ask May he said okay, he would wait for an answer.

I had gone home from school I told May that there was a guy in my science class that had asked me out on a date, she then would say you know my feelings about dating in school I said yes I did remember what you had said, William had walked up and said there is no harm in going to the movies with a young man.

They, May and William started arguing about me dating May would come back in and say, go on the date this weekend you will leave here at seven and be back at nine, so whatever movie you can find to see in those hours is fine.

May would also go on to say after the date she would check me to see if I had sex with this person.

I would have to lie down on the dining room table in front of everyone while I would be checked I said I understood everything that was said to me.

The next day I went to school my stomach was a little upset, Katherine and D.D. asked me what was said I told them that May had said yes but I was going to be checked after the date, and that I had agreed to that.

They told me that May was sick and had some sort of perversions and she was just taking them out on me, I agreed a few hours later in science class I would tell Lindsey the answer was yes, Lindsey smiled with a soft smile on his kind face and said okay, we will just go to a movie until eight forty five and then he would bring me home.

Saturday was here I was dressed up and ready to go I felt very nervous, I had never been on a real date before alone with an older teenager than I, what would I do if he touched me in the wrong way would I scream, maybe hit him what? Yes, my stomach was very upset

I did not know what to look forward to, it's time I saw Lindsey pull up and he is knocking on the door.

I came down stairs my sisters say how nice I looked, which built up my confidence just a little and then we left. Lindsey told me that the car belonged to his parents and that he had to be really careful with it. We would get to the drive-in movies "The Car" was playing.

Lindsey would get snacks while I waited in the car, we watched some of the movie about an hours worth and then we left we just drive around, Lindsey wanted to just get to know me, he would tell me that he knew my brother Michael, I thought that was cool, he would go on to say they were good friends and he liked playing football with him.

Time was up two hours goes by so quickly I had nothing to worry about Lindsey was great.

The date was over time for me to show up at home to get the third degree maybe even have to lie down and spread my legs to prove that I did not have sex, which was stated be fore I had gone on the date.

In the car in front of the house Lindsey gave me a kiss on the lips a tender kiss barley touching his lip to mine, I thought that was okay as did Lindsey, we both got out of the car and walked to the front door side by side,

Lindsey said hello to Michael, whom answered the door Lindsey and I walked into the house, to meet my parents and Michael followed.

May was in the living room sitting on the couch the first room that you come to entering the house; May was lying across Williams lap with just her bra and panties on.

Lindsey didn't know what to say he apologized for walking in on something he shouldn't have, William looked up and said hello May woke up and started yelling get out, over and over again.

I don't know why May was dressed like this William would say, and he had apologized to Lindsey, I walked Lindsey out and I told him I would see him on Monday at school.

He said he was sorry for walking in on whatever was going on I told him I knew as much as he knew, that wasn't much at this time in May's life she weighed about two hundred and fifty pounds, at that weight I would not be caught dead in just panties and a bra, she was showing everything plus what would not fit in her bra and panties.

I thought that was the most disgusting thing to see, May naked as you bring your date home to meet the family, especially when I was told that Lindsey was to walk to the door leaving and coming home from the date.

May started to yell at me which I didn't know why, I was not in the wrong I was not the one just sitting on the couch looking like a large animal wearing just a bra and panties, she knew I was to be home soon, she should have had the decency to at least put on a robe but as usual, it was never her fault it was always mine, or someone else's fault, just not May's.

May had made me sit at the table while sitting there I was called a bitch and a slut, even a whore that night whatever name May be able to think of that is what I was to her, I was blamed for everything even being born.

I guess it was not really unnatural for us as May always walked around the house half naked on a daily basis, either no top just a bra, or no pants just panties.

Why not let people see what we had to see on a daily basis.

There was no real reason for her to dress that way, other than that is the way she dressed.

For my first date it now was the date from hell, May had asked did he touch you, I said no he did not; he was a very nice person. It really seemed hard for her to believe that there were really nice people in the world. She walked over to me, grabbed my breast, and said did he do that? Once again I said no. I was again called a liar, as May motioned to hit me William walked into the room, May had instructed me to go to bed, would take care of me in the morning.

I thought to myself, why not now, is it because William is home. Most all of our beatings took place while William was at work, just because he did not like how May treated us as children.

Arlene D. Arnold

The next day was almost the last

It was Sunday morning I woke up I heard talking downstairs and I just wanted to stay in my room, I had heard May say to who ever was down stairs at the time tell that bitch to come downstairs, I knew she was talking about me, my sisters came up to get me and let me know she was mad, I knew.

I walked downstairs and was told to sit at the table I did, I was yelled at for about ten minutes I was told that was the last and only date I would go on, May said to me do you understand I replied said yes.

May did not like how I answered her she grabbed me by my t- shirt and slapped me as hard as she could knocking me down to the floor, before I could get up her foot was on my chest and she was still calling me names, she treated me worse than you could ever treat a dog that day I was let up off the floor to wash the dishes.

She had gone somewhere else in the house I had walked into the kitchen grabbed a dirty steak knife and shoved it against my stomach.

The point of the dirty knife hurt as I pushed it against my abdomen, I thought to myself this will not work I wanted to die but I did not want to feel the pain if I would die I would not have to go through this hell ever again.

Remembering my childhood the years of being raped over and over again, all of the abuse from both Jay and May, the beatings that I just did not deserve nor did the rest of my brothers and sisters, then as I washed the dishes I was thinking the whole time how to end it all and then it came to me a razor blade.

I walked into the bathroom and grabbed one of Williams's razor blades and left the house, I had made it to the railroad tracks crying and sobbing.

I pulled out the razor blade from my pocket and quickly ran it across my wrist it did not hurt, it just stung a little I was bleeding just a little so I did it again and just kept walking down the tracks.

Blood started dripping rapidly to the tips of my fingers, there was blood all over my bright yellow t-shirt and down the front of my rust colored pants, I was dizzy from crying I thought I was going to faint.

I wanted to see God I was ready I was not afraid to die my pain would be over, I came to an intersection where the Menlo Park train station would be, I kept walking and then I saw flashing lights, it was an officer that I had gone on a ride along with.

She gotten out of her car and walked over to me not to close though she did not know my state of mind all she knew was I had blood on me and I was crying, I just wanted to keep walking and I did as the officer followed me asking me the whole time what was wrong? I said I did not want to be on this earth anymore, she asked if I would walk with her I said no, it was my time to be by myself and I did not want to go home nor did I want May to be called the officer had called for help.

The officer had said if I had come with her she would take me to the hospital to get fixed up and that I would not have to go home if I did not want to, the officer had already known May and as I was taken into the hospital I guess she was called.

A doctor had come into the room I was in he would ask me many questions and I would just pretend he was not there I had blanked him out.

The doctor had left the room and May had walked in right at that moment I said to myself, I could never trust anyone my faith and trust were now gone in everyone.

May had told me if I did not talk I would be going to another hospital to stay she said those words with no care or emotion, it was almost like she was being made to say what she did like a robot, trying to be the good mother in someone's eyes.

That was really fine with me I did not want to go back to that hellhole I was instructed by May to tell the doctors that I was slapped because of something I had done wrong that's it nothing more or less, I stayed quiet as the doctor came in and stitched my wrist up.

May would be sitting there the whole time watching everything, the doctor had finally asked her to leave the room, and another doctor came in and I did as I was told when asked again.

Why did you do that to yourself, I decided to tell him the whole story not May's story, I had told him that May had slapped me and I fell to the floor and when I hit the floor May stood on my chest and would not let me up.

The night before I had gone on a date with a classmate and when I arrived home he had come into the house and saw her in just her bra and panties, and the next day May had taken her abuse out on me.

The hospital as well as the doctor had allowed me to go home, one of the physicians I was given a number if this was to ever happen again, and the number was given to me in front of May, even though I did not want to go home with May I had to, but things would be different now.

On the way home May had said to me, "why didn't you cut yourself deeper", I will never forget how hateful she was, she would also say how much I embarrassed her.

May would then say next time make sure you do it right I had nothing to say to her during the ride home, I just sat there and pretend not to hear a word she would say.

We had pulled into the driveway at home I was told to just go to my bedroom by May, would the say I just don't want to see you, not at all.

To my room I went sat on my bed and just wondered why God had wanted me to stay, what were his plans for me, what were my reasons to go on living? I had just sat there on my bed thinking to myself, was May going to leave me alone now?

My sister had come into the bedroom, they both said I had scared them, and as much as I hated it there, I would be out of this house soon, so don't do anything to hurt myself ever again.

I had thought about what my sisters had said the promise was made asked God, as you see my pain and suffering, why do you let May do this to our family? Why wont you help us? Just make her leave.

The next day would be school I couldn't wait to get there either; I wanted to talk to Katherine and D.D. so bad.

Monday

Katherine and D.D. had walked up to me they were so excite for me my first real date, Katherine would say well how did it go don't keep us in suspense, and tell us, I broke down and just started to cry, I did not want to remember this past weekend, not at all.

Both Katherine and D.D. would say oh my God what happened, seeing my wrist in a bandage, we sat on the grass in front of the school, where we always sat and I told them both what happened. May is just trying to kill you, that are what it sounds like to us, they would both say.

It was time for science class, how was I going to face Lindsey? Lindsey had come over to me and asked if I were okay, he would then tell me that my brother had told me what happened.

Your mother is such a bitch, Lindsey said, he also had fun on our date until the end, and he would never forget me and that was the end of Lindsey, which was for the best; I did not need anything else in my life right now.

I did not want Lindsey to think any of this was his fault, he'll be okay, but would I?

Katherine and D.D. went to all of my classes with me, teary eyed, they were both sad for me, and I could see it in their faces.

My teachers also had known what happened they would just tell me to call for help next time, don't hurt myself.

At the end of the school day Katherine said she was walking home with me, and if May had said anything to me or her she would let her have it, telling her exactly what kind of person she really thought she was, telling her off. We arrived home and no one was there Katherine had stayed with me and help with the folding of my new papers, and the her mother had come and picked her up.

Katherine said as she was leaving just stay away from her as much as possible, I would reply by saying okay, I did my route with my brother came home and just stayed in my room, I did not say a word to May, nor did she say anything to me.

Christmas vacation was coming which I dreaded I would be home,

No friends to talk to, I did have my brother Michael, whom hated May with a passion, and my sisters though.

Arlene D. Arnold

A few days before Christmas Vacation

I had bought gifts to school for Katherine and D.D., as they both had done for me, they had both said during the vacation if anything happened at home to call one of them, and they would try to help as best they could, I agreed, well it is Christmas vacation, what am I going to do for two weeks.

Just the usual, my route and clean house was about what I had to look forward to.

Christmas was not really celebrated not any more, we didn't even set up a Christmas tree, I thought to my self why would we any way, this is not a family by no means, and I did not even really know what a real family was suppose to act like.

I had glimpses of some of my friend's families in the past, and they seemed happy, was it real happiness, I just don't know.

Christmas had come and gone. I bought gifts for my sisters and brother, as did they. The holidays

For this family was a farce, fake, just not real, not for me any way.

Gifts from May were few, mostly for William, and that was okay. William would be the one to stick around, surly not any of us children.

During the vacation, I had no words with May at all, She would say what she wanted done, and I would do it.

William would ask me from time to time how I was doing, I thought to myself why do you care, because most of the time he didn't seem to say much, whether May was beating us or not.

I did feel sorry for William though, I thought that he was suffering just like us, but just could not see or did not want to see the abuse; I did like William's music that he would play though, Classical, Opera, and Jazz.

The Classical and Opera music both had sometimes made me sad, depending on the composer, the other music William played was very upbeat, and happy.

I, myself was thinking that the sad music that was playing meant William was upset about something, like me when he played the music I would feel upset or sad, the upbeat music was happiness, and William would be happy, that is what I saw and heard anytime music was played.

When May was there, and the music was played, there was always yelling and total chaos, she did not like the music at all she hated listening to it, I remember when he would pull all of the stereo equipment and wires out of the wall, almost on a weekly basis.

What was wrong with May, could she not let anyone that has crossed her path be happy? She is such a hateful person, how did God release her to this world? I had thought that to myself constantly, I also had thought if God had know how many lives May has ruined, or has tried to ruin, would God have still let her come into this world? There are so many unanswered questions, that I have asked God, which I have yet to have answered.

Vacation is over, back to my friends, and the normalcy I have come to know out side of the home.

January

I had gone back to school the vacation was over if that is what it was suppose to be, I felt so much stress after what had happen to me a few months ago, I sill was not over that ordeal, I was happy to see my friends though, they were a comfort to my eyes and my heart and my soul, Katherine had asked me if anything had happened on the vacation, I answered, not one thing. May does not even really talk to me, she relays all messages to my brothers and sisters, they now give me my orders relayed by May, May has always involved us children in her cruelty and punishments.

Both Katherine and D.D. said that was better than her harassing me, just taunting me with her verbal abuse, I said yes but I did not like her torture my younger brother and sisters that way.

It was now time to sign up for new semester classes, and I still wanted nine classes, but I would not be able once again to take them all with Katherine and D.D. I signed up with as many classes I could with the both of them, science, math, history, and phys Ed, with Katherine.

I remember phys Ed being such a tough class for me, mostly the running, my leg that I had broke a few years earlier just hurt badly, every time I had jumped or ran, I did the best that I could do, I did tell May my leg had hurt in phys Ed, she just said what do you want me to do about it? I said nothing.

Why did I even bother to say anything to her about my pain? She was the cause of most of it, and why would she even care. That was really stupid on my part.

I had slowly been gaining weight since the eighth grade, I did not know why, I exercised every day in school, and at home with my route, riding my bike all of the time. I did not understand why.

So my leg would stop hurting me, I along with Katherine had decided to take jazz dance, and weight management class.

To pass the class we had three months to loose ten pounds, part of phys ed, we had loss the weight, one of the greatest classes to have in high school a long with swimming, my leg still hurt me but the class was easier to deal with other than running all of the time.

February, Parent and teacher conferences were here and school was letting out early, if the class that I was to go to was, closed due to conferences I was allowed to go home, I had never told May about early dismissal from school if school was not in for me that day, Katherine, D.D., and I would decide were we would go for at least six hours.

Katherine would say to me lets go to San Francisco, we all agreed, bought a train ticket and went, the first time we had gone to San Francisco, just the three of us, I was so scared, what would happened if I was caught leaving the school, or something happened to me in San Francisco. I soon was over that, the fear of being in trouble, what could happen, death?

We had gone to Fisherman's Warf, had seafood, and went to museums on the Warf; we just had fun, fun that I had never experienced before, life was worth living, just not in the home I was living in.

March was here

My birthday was here I was not really looking forward to it, and the day had just snuck up on me, I had gone to school, Katherine and D.D. were waiting for me, and conferences were still going on, lets go meet my mother Katherine would say, I said okay, while we were waiting for the bus, Katherine had given me a birthday gift, as did D.D., they both had made me feel so special.

We hopped on a bus and we were at Katherine's mother's restaurant, there Katherine's mother made us burgers and fries, then I went to Katherine's home to see how she lived, Katherine had such a peaceful environment.

I wished that we were sisters, like everyone thought we were wished I were going home from school with her every day.

Just a wish, just a dream, I could never leave my brother and sisters there with that witch to fend for them selves, although she seemed to be getting easier on them.

I had a great day one of the best birthdays in a long time, thank you Katherine and D.D. for making that day special for me.

It was time to go home there was nothing special about that, a box on the counter, make your own cake was not a special birthday.

I went home did my route, and just wanted to go to bed to get ready for the next day.

There was no cake on the counter to make, so I did not have to do that.

I went upstairs to go to bed, and I was asked by William to come down stairs, I said okay, I came down stairs and he had put on a sweet sixteen song for me, which I thought was nice.

I went into the dining room and there was a lit cake, store bought, I was asked by William to sit down and blow out the candles but make a wish first, I did, from my brothers and sister I would receive John Denver Albums, May said she had bought the cake, and her and William had decided to take me to a French restaurant for my *sixteenth birthday.*

I received several gifts from William, a Tambourine, because I like music so much, and my first book called "The Prophet" By Kahlil Gibran 1883-1931 a poet, philosopher, and artist, he was filled with expressions heart and the mind.

This would become one of the most important gifts I had received of all. I would read it constantly over the years, and remember everything Gibran had said in The Prophet about children, this is what he had said about children here are his quotes.

"Your children are not your children.
They are the sons and daughters of Life's longing for itself.

They come through you but not from you,
And though they are with you, yet they belong not to you.
You may give them your love but not your thoughts.
For they have their own thoughts.
You may house their bodies but not their souls,
For their souls dwell in the house of tomorrow,
which you cannot visit, not even in your dreams."

By Kahlil Gibran

I would tell William how much sense this book had made to me, and the best part was "*your children are not your children*", Gibran was correct in his thinking, I never did belong to anyone, but I was sure made to feel different.

"They come through you but not from you, and though they are with you, yet they belong not to you".

The last statement I felt to be true also, I was born not for abuse, or someone else's pleasures, although I felt like I was a pleasure toy, a game piece.

"You may give them your love but not your thoughts. For they have their own thoughts."

I never felt loved, but I was always given thoughts that I did not believe in or agree with, I had my own thoughts, but was never allowed to voice them, never.

"You may house their bodies but not their souls, for their souls dwell in the house of tomorrow, which you cannot visit, not even in your dreams."

My body was housed, abused, molested, raped and my soul taken from me, the house of tomorrow would seem like a lifetime to get my soul back or search for my inner self.

Tomorrow has come along time ago, May will never be allowed to visit me, in reality, but I have not been able to get her out of my dreams, or my thoughts, as a matter of fact, I can't get rid of Jay either, I always try not to go backwards, and dwell on yesterdays, I strive to find a happy future, It has been a struggle; I am not there yet, but some day.

If you would like to learn more about Kahlil Gibran, please consult your local library, or bookstore here are more books by Kahlil Gibran

Thank you William, this book has made a great impact on my life, and it always will, the gift that will last a lifetime, I had gone to dinner, a French restaurant, came home and went to bed.

I had gone back to school the next day, I had told Katherine and D.D. about the book I had received, even showed it to them, it was over their heads, they did not understand it like I did, that was okay, I did not want to force anything on the both of them that they did not want to hear, they both were just happy that I had not suffered any misery, and that my birthday had gone well.

As for the rest of March, it went okay without any incidents. I would go to school, be with my friends, come home and do my route, clean, read my new book and the next day I would write in my diary at school.

I was now sixteen and able to take drivers education three months had past, and now I was able to get my drivers license, I was taken to the DMV by May, and allowed to get my license. On the written portion of the test I missed two questions, and on the driving I missed nothing I now had a license.

For what reason was I allowed having a license, of course it was to make sure the cars had gas in them at all times.

Pay bills for May, and pick up whatever May needed, when she wanted it. That's why I was allowed to have a license.

It was now June and school would now be out for a few months, I would miss my friends a lot, what did this summer hold for me? Would there be more punishment for just living, I did not know what was in store for me, I sure did wonder though.

At sixteen years old, I wondered to myself if I was pretty, my brother Michael always said I looked good, but he was my brother, and he always tried to make me feel good about myself.

Being on the paper route together everyday, Michael would meet all kinds of guys at the boy's college, when we would do the complete paper route together, he would introduce me to some of his friends. They would tell me that I was good looking also, that made me feel good about myself also. Not that the words came from a guy, just that I was told that I looked good.

I was introduced by my brother Michael to a guy named Terry, whom lived at the college in one of the dorms. I would talk to Terry everyday during the summer. I was sixteen, and one day Terry told me that he could not associate with anyone under the age of eighteen.

Terry asked me how old I was, I had thought about what he said earlier, I replied eighteen, he said okay and a week had past and I was still talking to Terry, when I saw a schoolmate at the dorm, she new me, she asked what I was doing there? I said I was visiting a friend.

Terry had just opened his door as my schoolmate said; does he know how old you are? I said I told him I was eighteen, she said you are only sixteen though, Terry told me to leave, I had told him the only reason I had said I was eighteen, is because that is what he wanted to hear, I left, never to talk to or see him again.

I would spend the rest of the summer just thinking.

Just thinking

I was able to have some peace and quiet, by saying peace; I was not bothered by May too much now, she had not much to say to me I never felt comfortable around her alone, deep down inside she scared me; I thought that she was a deranged and sick person, she really never needed to have children, not with the suffering and abuse she had put me and my brothers and sisters through.

Well we must go on with our lives, the best way possible, try not to look back at the bad and move on towards the future, what would be in store for me this up and coming year as a junior in high school, there was not many more credits needed to graduate, I mostly needed elective classes, what if I just could not handle being at home any more, what if I just had to leave?

There were so many thoughts going through my mind at this time, where would I go, if I had decided to leave, just move out with just what I could carry, I sure didn't have a good plan at all, I did my paper route and my chores, and just went to my room to think.

I looked at the flowers on my bedroom wall, just the colors and the way they were arranged, so perfect so just right what would I want to be when I grew up?

I really did not know as I did not know who I was anymore I really wanted to go into the Navy, just to follow through with my dreams, have a career, but that would not happen for me, they would not take me because I was such a confused person, I did not like men much either, and men would pretty much be authority figures.

For me at that time in my life it would be just too hard to look up to any man, I now have fuzzy thinking, fuzzy because, I used to know what I wanted out of life, but think so much about the past, what could I have done differently?

Maybe I could have been born to a more loving family, my father excluded from these thoughts because he had no choices, just like me, maybe I could have just died at birth, and just prevented misery altogether, there is an answer in my being, and God knows why, he has a plan, I just have to wait and see what the future has in store for me I guess.

While I am waiting I still need a plan, the great plan, and the great escape, how and when will this take place, which was there to help me?

Daily thinking is just driving me crazy, I wanted to get away from May; she is just unhealthy for me and has been for a long time, If I stay here I will probably just end up dead, which sometimes I think how easy it is, I would go so peacefully.

Those thoughts come and go all of the time as I said earlier, what is happy?

It is almost time for the big return to school summer has seemed to go by so quickly, maybe that is because May is just leaving me alone, I am so much more at peace when she is not around.

May, sometime tries to be friendlier, is it because that is what William wanted her to do? It is too late to take back what she can't give back; I will never smile around her, for what? To say that I forgive her for everything that she has done, or allowed to be done to me, I will never forgive May or give her the satisfaction of forgiveness ever I would rather be dead.

Well, it is one week before the start of the new school year; it is time to get my wardrobe ready with what funds I have acquired.

As I said earlier my money is not my money, the money I make is dished out to me in bits and parts, mostly bits, I get to have a hundred dollars, but I made over a thousand this summer, I never ask why, what for? It would just mean some sort of tortuous abuse; I would have to make do with what was given to me.

I bought a few pairs of pants, and a few tops, this would have to last me at least six months, before I would get another hundred dollars for the next six months.

Tomorrow is the first day of my junior year.

Junior Year 1978`

The first day back to school I would see my friends Katherine and D.D., they looked great in their new clothes, I could not compare to them, well any way that didn't matter much to those two my best friends, we were just so happy to be able to hang out with each other again.

The first thing we did was to see how many classes we would be able to take together, and once again I took nine, as many credit as I could get, mostly elective classes, which made going to school a lot more fun, two art, one of my favorite subjects, two classes in jewelry making, R.O.T.C., typing, home economics, history, and phys Ed.

Katherine and D.D. were in just about all of my classes, this was really hard to do, but we did it.

Under the oak tree in front of the school we would discuss our summer vacation.

Both Katherine and D.D. were very anxious to hear about my summer, anything juicy Katherine would say. I am so sorry to say, I did not get hit, slapped, not even yelled at once.

What happened D.D. would say is she sick, I don't know what is wrong with her maybe she realizes that I am leaving soon maybe she is just wrapped up in herself and William, her boyfriend I just don't know.

We left campus at lunchtime we went to Palo Alto, where Katherine's bank was, and she wanted me to open an account, somewhere I could place my tip money from my route, since I had to give the rest of my money to May, I now had my first account at a bank, wow I thought this was great.

Weekly we would go to the bank at lunchtime and put money into my account, and do a little shopping, I remember going to the Gap to get a pair of pants to wear just like Katherine's, we would eat lunch, and then go back to school.

The first day of March it was my birthday

A few months had gone by and I was really tired of going on a paper route every day, not really going on the route, and seeing people that I would see daily, but just carrying the heavy news papers.

One of my classes in school was work experience, I had to go out and fill out applications, and get a job, and I did. I was now working at McDonald's near home, I received a paycheck weekly I had to give May half of the check, and the other half I was able to keep and it went into my account.

One day my bike tires were low on air I went to the gas station around the corner from our house, I would be filling up my tire and this guy named Bob had come over to me and say would you like some help he would say, I said sure he was very nice and after school each day I would get air, and Bob would help.

I recall Bob asking me if I would go on a date with him, I would say that he would have to ask May, which he had also known from filling up her car all of the time, and seeing us both together.

Bob had shown up at the door one day, May answered the door asked what he wanted; he replied, "I am here to ask you if I can take out you daughter Arlene"?

May asked him into the house she had given him the third degree, Bob was ten years older than I was she then gave him the okay.

Saturday I would get to go to the movies again what would happen this time?

Would I be told the same thing I would be checked to see if I had sex? Or, would May just start beating on me because she did not like to wear clothing around the house, it really did not matter if we saw her half naked, but it did matter if someone else outside of the home saw her naked.

I really did not want to go through the same hell as I did before; I did not want to go to the movies, just because of the memories of what happened last time.

I had let Bob know what my feelings were on the matter, and he said that was okay we could go anywhere I wanted to go, I chose swimming and he said okay.

The reason I chose swimming was because I knew that I didn't have to be close to this person, Bob.

Although I have bad memories from that as well what was I going to do go through life not being able to do anything? As it was I did not like to be touched by a man, I thought I would never get over that, which I really have not. It is very hard to be in the same room with a man, unless I am several feet away from him, I have to really get to know the person before I feel that I can let my guard down.

I am just thinking again, what if Bob wants to have sex he is ten years older than I am what am I going to, he is a nice person; he could be the one, the one to help me escape form the hellish torment that I have to live through on a daily basis.

I ask God what should I do but he does not answer me, I guess I am on my own, fend for myself, why couldn't I have a happy childhood. Is there an easier way out, do I have to give myself to someone just to leave the hell that I am living?

There is always another choice, I could kill myself, and I would not have to worry about anything ever again, I am so confused on what to do.

I tell Katherine and D.D. what is going through my head at school the next day, Katherine said I want to meet this person, and she did at lunchtime, after lunch was over and we were back at school, she said to me, you can do so much better, but he could be a way out.

I asked Katherine if I should have sex with Bob, she said that she couldn't help me there, knowing your background with sex, how easy is that going to be for you to do?

I could just close my eyes and pretend that I just wasn't there I would be numb to the fact that he was even touching me, I just want out of the hell I am living in, Katherine would say, I will not say for you to do it, the choice are yours, and you can still find someone better than that. Today is Friday, I am not ready for tomorrow, I need sleep, and maybe I will see things differently when I wake up, maybe.

The first day of March was tomorrow; I would be seventeen years old, nothing all that special, cake, ice cream, that's pretty much it here at home.

At school, Katherine and D.D. always tried to make my day special for me, we ate lunch off campus, had ice cream, and I was given gifts, these two friends are the best people that you could ever have in your life. Life is always happy when they are around.

I would hope that I would leave such a strong impression on their lives as they did mine.

Saturday is here, another date

I did my chores in the morning when I woke up just so I did not have to hear right before the date, you did not do this or that and about noontime I started to worry about what was going to happen later this evening, what if I had to do something I did not want to do, I had to gain confidence in, and let Bob feel like I really did like him, what is like? What is love? I did not know either one of those things, how was I to know any one of those thinks, I did not have like, and love in my life.

About three o'clock, I felt ill, just thinking over and over again, what is going to happen this evening? Time started moving more rapidly; it was now five in the early evening, May never said a word to me, not one, It was now six and Bob was at the door, knocking. May had clothes on wow, and answered the door she would ask Bob to come in and he did, walking into the dining room, he would wait for me to come downstairs, I came down stairs and said hello to Bob, I was asked if I was ready to go I said yes.

May then spoke I want her back in this house no later than eleven this evening.

Bob had agreed and we started walking towards the front door Bob opened the door and we walked out to the car, got in and drove of into the sunset.

We drove to a cove in Redwood City a cove where you could go swimming I was already wearing my swimsuit, as was Bob under our clothing.

We arrived at the little cove undressed and went out to the water to go swimming, the water was warm after a nice warm day, we swam for about two hours, the walked out of the water to get dried off.

We put on our clothes over our swimming suits and walked to the car, we tried to get into the car and we were unable to Bob thought he left the keys on the beach, he didn't and they were locked inside the car with his wallet now what?

It was about eight thirty in the evening and nothing was open, we walked to me closest Hotel to make some calls to locksmiths, we had no luck, we then called a towing company, and they came out and unlocked the car. It was now nine thirty in the evening the date was going okay, it would now take almost a half an hour to get back home and it would be ten at night, we made it, we had an hour to kill so we sat in the car near the house and just talked.

Bob would say how nice he thought I was and we would discuss May, and what kind of person she is, how I wanted to leave home and never look back, Bob said with time that would happen.

I was aloud to date Bob on a regular basis now every weekend, or every other weekend, we would either go out to eat diner or swim or just watch TV.

Bob a hard working mechanic, what does he see in me, all I know is that he likes me and May seems to like him around, she has no problem with him.

She never yelled when he was around again trying to be someone she wasn't, the kind sweet person other people knew but I knew differently.

Arlene D. Arnold

My Junior Prom

I had two weeks before the prom and I did not want to go with just anyone who asked me, and I wanted to be with friends, this created a heated argument again between May and myself. She wanted me to experience other guys in my life; she wanted me to go with other boys in my class, instead of my friends.

I said to solve the problem I just wont go I was slapped for that by May, she would say you will go with who ever I say for you to go with and you are going. That was the end of the discussion. She would say and further more, you will not be dating Bob any more, and then she just walked away.

I went to my room and just cried I cried so long my eyes were puffy and I could barely see out of them.

William walked by my bedroom door and asked me what happened, I told him that May had slapped me and told me that I was to go to the prom with whom she chose for me to go with. I also told him I was no longer allowed to go out with Bob.

William told me to dry my tears he would talk with May about the prom, but he did not have much to say about Bob, I said okay.

William went downstairs and all I heard was arguing and yelling and screaming from both May and William. May walked upstairs and said look what you have caused, again. You go to your prom with who ever you want, but Bob is no longer allowed around this house, and May turned around and walked out of the room. She said out loud, I wish I never had you, and in my mind I said to myself, I wish the same.

I went to school and there was prom talk everywhere and Katherine and D.D. were given the news I am allowed to go to the prom and I will be able to go with the both of you, we huddled up together and gave each other a big hug.

Now we had to decide what to where for that special evening the theme for the prom was summer breeze.

With the money I had saved up I went shopping with Katherine, she wanted a white long gown and I wanted a blue one, which looked similar to the one she wanted, at lunchtime we would go to the Mall in Palo Alto, just to try on gowns.

We had both found the gowns that we were looking for and,

Katherine bought hers and I told her I would be back to get mine.

That would not be true I had asked May for some of my money from work so that I could go pick up my prom dress, she said no we would both be going to the Mall together, and I will choose your dress. I didn't argue with her, I just went. At this point in time I really did not care what I was wearing as long as I was going to the prom.

May chose a pail blue dress the gown was satin with see through lace covering the top of the gown, I liked it, as it did look very nice, not what Katherine and I chose together, but it will work.

The next day at school I told Katherine I was unable to get the dress that we had both chose, but I did get a nice one is it still blue Katherine would ask, I said yes? I ask Katherine why she asked that she said that D.D. is buying the corsages. I told he that was very nice.

I just hope nothing happens before our big night out like May saying I could not go, something like that, Katherine assured me I would be going to the prom.

A few days to go I can't wait to see all of my classmates dresses up, I can't wait to see Katherine and D.D., Katherine in a white gown, and D.D. in a pale blue tuxedo.

The prom is here my hair had to be done and I was taken to the beauty salon by May, to have my hair done, as I was paying for it. I was there for about two hours, my hair turned out great, with many curls. May had picked me up and did not like my hair at all.

We went home my hair was re-done, washed and curled by May, and then she would say that is how your hair should look, my hair was up, with many curls dangling down to my shoulders. I was just not going to get mad, that is what it seemed like May wanted.

For me to get upset or for her to get upset at me, a reason, any reason not to go to the prom. She never went to her prom, and I think she regrets not going. May wants to go to the prom though me, it is my turn, she had her chance, I would say to my self.

Arlene D. Arnold

Prom Night

The month was April and the year nineteen Seventy-Eight the theme for the evening was Summer Breeze.

My hair was done and I had my stockings and dress to put on and I would be ready to go.

It is six in the evening I am walking upstairs to get ready for my big night the biggest night of the year.

I sit on the edge of my bed just think how this evening will end up, and I say to myself everything will be fine, I start to slide on my stockings rolling them up so slowly so that I don't put a run in them, they are on and now for my dress, I don't want to mess up my hair.

The zipper on the dress zips all the ways down to were my waist would be. I slide my dress on, and my sister zips me up and tells me how beautiful I am. I tell Brenda thank you and say I hope everyone else feels the same way.

I stand and look into the mirror and I see a young lady in a very nice pale blue dress with sheer light blue lace for my sleeves and the neckline, pretty, almost like a princess, ready for an evening out on the town.

There is a knock on the front door and it is my friend D.D., and I slowly walk downstairs to greet him. I say hello and introduce him to May and William.

D.D. was wearing a pale blue tuxedo; he looked very handsome, from head to toe.

D.D. was carrying a beautiful gardenia corsage, still in its clear blue case. D.D. opens the clear case, takes out the corsage, and places it on my wrist.

I thought to myself what a wonder thing to do for me and the flower had a very beautiful fragrance also. D.D. asked me if I was ready to go, I said yes, he then asked May what time I had to be home, very politely. May answered, I don't want Arlene home no later than 5am, D.D. smiled and said okay.

We were followed outside to see a black Limo waiting, Katherine was waiting inside the limo for me, and she didn't have anything to say to May.

We arrive to the car door and D.D. opened the car door like a perfect gentleman.

Wow, I really do feel like a princess, and I was getting into the carriage with another princess. This is going to be a great evening.

We would now head to the ball; I mean the hotel wear the prom was being held at. We arrived, pulling up to the front of the hotel, our doors were opened for us, and we stepped out of the car like we were stars for the evening.

Walking into the hotel, classmates were getting their pictures taken, so we stood in line to do the same. Snap, our pictures were taken, one together as a group, and the one by ourselves, and then one with the gentleman that had brought you to the prom.

That was done, not hard at all. We would now all hold hands walking into the large ballroom, we did it, we are here we would all yell. We were ushered to our table.

We sat down for a small something to eat, then there was dancing, laughter, happiness, and joy. I looked around at the whole room; gold satin curtains hanging, a nice stage with a wonderful band, and balloons everywhere.

The tables had white satin table clothes; with napkins it was just perfect.

We were here for about two hours, and then we left for the beaches of San Francisco.

We arrived at the beach in San Francisco at about ten in the evening we would end up near The Cliff House, coast highway one. Then travel to the beach area where we stopped the car, we would now take off our shoes and get out of the car and run in the sand and then sit down and watch the waves come in and go out.

It was just one of the greatest nights of my life, Katherine asked me what did I think I was going to do when I was finally out of school? I said why, she said let's go to college together I said that would be great, I really loved Katherine and D.D. for making this night happen, we sat here for about two hours just talking about the future, and what it would be like to always be together.

It was getting a little cold, so we sat in the car, and D.D. had a bottle of champagne and glasses, we toasted to the evening, and the future.

Then we went to breakfast we looked great walking into the restaurant, everyone holding hands and we're a team, my best friends, I will never forget the both of you, you made me live, and have shown me what happiness could be like.

We sat down and had breakfast and then just sat and talked some more mostly about the evening and how great is was, it is about one thirty in the morning and we decide to go back to the beach have a little more champagne, and just watch the waves. The night seemed to be just rushing by; I wished that it never ended. We stayed here until two-thirty in the morning, then it was time to start back, as it took forty-five minutes or longer to get home.

An hour later I arrived home D.D. open my car door like a gentleman again, walked me to the door and gave me a kiss on the cheek, once again I thanked him and Katherine for the greatest evening, then said goodnight.

I went upstairs to my room took off my clothes and jumped into bed and went to sleep, and dreamed about the wonderful evening I just had and how I wished it never ended. Goodnight.

The day after the prom was Saturday I was asked many questions but the bottom line was I, as well as D.D. and Katherine had fun.

At school my classmates would tell me how beautiful I looked at the prom and I would tell them the same, it was a very special time in our lives. The discussion at school would now be about prom night, for the rest of the school year, which has now come to an end, and summer vacation was here.

Summer of 78

Well I would not get to see D.D. and Katherine for a few months it was now working and maybe getting to see a movie or two with my brother Michael, one Saturday I did not have to work and Michael asked if I wanted to go and see a movie with him, I said yes.

The movie did not start until about five late in the afternoon Michael said lets go, we had both asked May prior to leaving and we started walking to the theater, we were almost half way there when the place where Michael was working had come up, a car lot where Michael detailed the cars, well he had the keys to one of the cars. He said come on lets go for a ride, and we did, Michael sat in the driver seat, and I was in the passenger side.

Michael took off, we pulled out of the parking lot driving very fast and crazy, we drove down the streets of Menlo Park and Atherton and then I wanted to drive so we switched seats, I took off and started to drive when I noticed a car honking in the rearview mirror.

Michael said go faster we can loose him and I did, we had hit speeds of one hundred miles an hour through town being chased, it was like we were in our own movie.

Being chased by the owner of the car for about a half an hour he had cut me off and I hit a brick wall as the car slid side ways into the wall.

Michael jumped out of the car and ran I was pulled out of the car by the owner as he was pulling me out he was choking me. He thought I was a boy; my hair was short, not passing me ears.

He put me in his car and took me back to the lot while driving back to the lot I was coughing up blood.

Michael finally showed up there asking if I was okay I said yes the police had arrived and were chasing after Michael, running in gravel it looked like slap stick comedy, Michael running one way then another making the officers fall to the ground, around in circles they went for about a good half hour.

Well they finally grabbed Michael we were both taken to juvenile hall, after sitting in the waiting room for May to show up I was let go and Michael had to stay because he had a prior history of getting in trouble.

Now I would have nobody at home to talk with, help me when I needed it, Michael was gone for one day of joy and fun with my brother, harmless fun no one was injured, Michael was now suffering but at least he was not at home to take the abuse that he would probably receive if he had come home.

Me on the other hand had to suffer the abuse a slap here yelled at there, how much more could I take in my life?

What now, I had to do 20 hours of community service I chose a nursing home to do my twenty hours, I remember the first day there at the nursing home my job was to read to the elderly people, in their rooms, I made many friends, there was one special lady I really liked, because she was sweet and kind, I read to her every day for two hours a day; on the fifth day back I would bring her cookies.

I walked into her room and the bed was empty I thought maybe I was in the wrong room I was not she had past away in her sleep I was told I started to cry, why did she have to go she was such a nice lady, she probably died of a broken heart because her family member never came to visit, she was very lonely and I would only be there a few more days, that was my first experience working with the elderly.

My community service was now over, which I thought to be a very good experience on the road to life some of life ups and downs and my experience of working with the elderly I thought to myself how could a family just throw away parents like that, then I looked at my life and my experience with my family. Was it like my life experience living with a woman whom had no care in the world to raise her children in a loving atmosphere, was that the case of this woman living in the nursing home or did her children just throw her away? My future, would it be working with the elderly? I didn't know.

Summer was almost over and I was now back at Mc Donald's working. I was there until summer came to a close.

I had to figure our what elective classes I wanted to take as I only needed Phys ED., and History.

I really could not wait to get back to school to see my friends, to talk over the summer, what had happen with Michael, and how I was now the only oldest child left at home.

Senior year 78' I left home, I was safe

This was a shaky start to the new school year, a guy named Bobby whom I new from school was in a very bad accident he was injured but his girlfriend died in the accident, I could remember calling Bobby several times because I didn't see him for a few days at school.

I remember telling Bobby that he had a lot to live for because he had said time and time again he did not want to live, a few days later I would call him and his parents told me that he was gone, I asked how and they told me that he shot himself and he was now gone, I felt so sad as this was announced over the schools PA system Bobby was now with his girlfriend.

Still shaken, I would just sit at school talking to Katherine and D.D. about the summer and what had happened with Michael and where he was and how I was the only oldest still at home and how uncomfortable I felt being here.

They had told me that their summer was very boring compared to mine, D.D. had then asked me how I manage to have such exciting vacations and we all laughed for a while and then stopped.

I said to Katherine "my life is shit." I want out of the house but there is no way out I work and my money goes to May for her to spend how she sees fit to spend it.

She might give me a small morsel of my money like five dollars if I gave her a good enough reason like personal items that a young lady might need.

Katherine said to me if at any time I need personal items like a young lady would need she would see that I had them. That was great I said, but it is so sad when you have to go to your friends for personal items, when I was working making my own money to buy these things for myself.

Katherine lightened up the subject and said, "What are friends for?"

A few weeks after school started I had only four classes, as did Katherine and D.D., and working after school I found time to see Bob as much as possible between school and work, without May gaining any knowledge of our meetings.

I started telling Bob a little more about my upbringing he felt sad for me and said if at anytime I needed to get away from home he would help me, I had agreed, and thank him for the offer.

A few days later I was in the kitchen with my sister and May, May was washing the dishes getting ready to canning fruit, I was asked by May to get up on a chair and to get a big pot down off the shelf so that she could start with canning I climbed up on a chair and May had a chain that you would lock your bike up with in her hands.

May said I was getting down the wrong pot and I said to her which pot do you want, well May didn't like how I said that she said "I don't like your tone of voice" and with the chain in her hand swung the chain very hard hitting me on my backside and my legs.

I was in pain I started to cry I took the pot down that she wanted and climbed off the chair put the chair back and I went upstairs and started packing my clothes, pulling everything off hangers putting them in my suitcase and pillowcases I put everything I was taking inside my closet.

I stayed in my room until I was called again by May, which I was two hours later she told me that I was to make diner and that she was going to a boy scout meeting with my younger brother, have it done by the time she came home, May was getting ready to leave and finally she left.

As soon as she was gone I called Bob at work to let him know I was ready to leave, I told him what happen earlier and he said to come and get the car, which was at work with him his job was only five minutes away from my home I put on my shoes and ran out the door.

I made it to Bob's place of work he gave me the keys and as fast as I could running up and down the stairs at home I loaded Bob's car, I drove to his apartment and then came back for some things of mine.

When I was done Bob asked me to pick him up from work and together we went back to his apartment.

I was such wreck by the time we had pulled up to Bob's apartment all I could do is cry, Bob told me that my life would be better now, now that I was away from home and that he, Bob would help me the best way he could.

A few days later there was a knock at the front door Bob was already gone for work and I was there in the apartment alone, very scared the mail drop was in the door all of a sudden mail came through the door and dropped to the floor my heart started beating again.

I went into the bathroom and just started to cry what was I going to do?

I was into the second quarter in school and I had my credits and if I quit now I just wont graduated with my senior class, at this point that was okay I really felt that I could not go on with school I just wanted to stay hidden, hidden from the outside world my friends, I could not tell them were I was because May would have gone to them first. I wanted to call Katherine so bad but I was told it was a bad idea and Bob said I just need some time to adjust to what was happening.

Day after day I sat in Bob's apartment no music, no television, just incase someone came over looking for me they would hear only silence.

A few more days had past and there was another knock at the door, I was in the living room the knock was now louder and then May's voice "Arlene if you are in there you better answer the door or I will have Bob arrested." I did not answer I just kept backing away from the door in the living room until I backed into the hallway, at that moment I could hear the mail flap opening and May saying the same sentence but louder.

I went into the bathroom because the window was too high up for anyone to look into, May finally left why does she want me home why? I will never go back to that place she calls home never.

Bob had come home and said he had a visit from May and she was looking for me I asked him did he say where I was he said no.

He did say that he had to get me out of the area away from her we had gone to his mother's house in San Francisco, Bob had changed his job to a different job in San Francisco and now I did not have to worry, I was left alone and Bob's mother treated me with respect she was a very nice woman with her own little quirks as we all have some, but nothing like May.

I was free, free from a life of living hell

My past was now in the past and in my future I had to reinvent my past as I did not and would not understand the people of the future would not either, I have to find a personality inside myself and for myself I need to build a future and tell people about the hell I was in as a child to adulthood, and in my heart that is why I believe that God has wanted me to go on with my life, to tell my story, to let children of past abuses know that the struggle of growing up in an abusive home can be endured and that evil can conquered.

As for sanity you really need to be around very loving people, people that can show you the other side of ugly, beauty.

I could not call Katherine or D.D., which made me very sad I was in a different world now my memories of the both of them would never be lost and I would always remember how they both helped me, made me stronger and helped me to see that there can be happiness, I escaped the hell I was living in and one day we will meet again.

271

There is so much more to my life the greatest thing of all is that I am still alive, I struggle with the memories of my past all of the time and one day I wont have to.

The future will be a struggle but there is no future like my past and I would wish my past on no human nor other walks of life as all are undeserving of the hell and torment I had to endure.

I wrote this book for my justice, justice in letting people that knew me and maybe even thought I was just a tad bit strange, well this book tells not all of the hell but most of what I could remember and I cannot regain those years but let me say that I have gone on with my life to the best of my ability.

Would I want justice yes but what can justice give back what was taken from my life?

Bring on the future and yet it is here.

About the Author

My name is Arlene Arnold; I currently live in Klamath Falls, Oregon with my husband Kenneth, and our two Schnauzers, Hans and Sebastian. This is where I chose to write my story.

This is a true story about my life as a survivor of sexual child abuse, incest and domestic violence. My book is detailed memories of my childhood to adulthood.

My greatest struggle was to leave the home I was in with some sanity, and my life, because everything else as you will read was pretty much taken from me.

This book is dedicated to others like myself, survivors of incest, rape, and child abuse.

Printed in the United States
41836LVS00001B/7

9 781403 355294